America in World Affairs ⚙

FOUNDATIONS OF AMERICAN GOVERNMENT
AND POLITICAL SCIENCE

Joseph P. Harris, Consulting Editor

The purpose of this series is to provide a group of relatively short treatises on major aspects of government in modern society. Each volume introduces the reader to a major field of political science through a discussion of important issues, problems, processes, and forces and at the same time includes an account of American political institutions. Each is the work of a distinguished scholar who is a specialist in and teaches the subjects covered. Together the volumes can well serve the needs of introductory courses in American government and political science.

ANDREW HACKER: The Study of Politics: The Western Tradition and American Origins

C. HERMAN PRITCHETT: The American Constitutional System

HUGH A. BONE and AUSTIN RANNEY: Politics and Voters

ROWLAND EGGER and JOSEPH P. HARRIS: The President and Congress

JOHN J. CORSON and JOSEPH P. HARRIS: Public Administration in Modern Society

CHARLES O. LERCHE, JR.: America in World Affairs

CHARLES R. ADRIAN: Governing Our Fifty States and Their Communities

AMERICA IN WORLD AFFAIRS

Charles O. Lerche, Jr.

Professor of International Relations
School of International Service
The American University

McGRAW-HILL BOOK COMPANY, INC.
NEW YORK / SAN FRANCISCO /
TORONTO / LONDON

AMERICA IN WORLD AFFAIRS

*This book is set in linotype Janson. The
original specimen sheets date from about
1700 and are of Dutch origin. The chapter
openings are Century Bold Condensed and
the displayed heads are News Gothic Bold.*

Preface

Something more than a nodding acquaintance with the exciting and pressing business of foreign affairs must be an integral part of the equipment of an effective American citizen today. No longer the exclusive province of specialists, the international relationships of the United States involve the security, the prosperity, and the very survival of everyone. The past two decades and more of American political life have been dominated by the problem of formulating and implementing the world role of the United States.

Citizenship in any active sense, therefore, now has an international dimension for Americans. The continued existence of the free and open society the United States has long epitomized demands that the "public"—however this term may be defined—perform its tasks both more knowledgeably and with a greater capacity for sophisticated analysis of world affairs.

The inclusion of this volume in a series on American government and political science reflects the new centrality of world affairs to Americans. This book is designed as an elementary guide to some of the fundamental considerations involved in American foreign policy. It is intended to be no more than an introduction; full understanding of and facility with its subject matter will of course require much more extensive study and application. But one must start somewhere, and the basic principles and data underlying a large subject usually furnish a useful foundation for subsequent mastery.

In general, this book attempts to avoid the vice of excessive contemporaneity. It is in no sense an inter-

pretation of recent newspaper headlines, but depends for its justification on whatever insights into the ongoing process of American foreign policy it might help to generate in its readers. The emphasis throughout, therefore, is more upon generalizations of reasonably broad applicability rather than upon detailed examination of particular situations and policies.

The book's six chapters fall into three more or less distinct groups. The first two attempt to analyze the world arena in which the United States moves, Chapter 1 considering the process of international politics and Chapter 2 examining the role of international organizations. Chapters 3 and 4 deal with two categories of factors that affect American action: the history of American foreign policy and the governmental mechanisms for the formulation and execution of policy. The last two chapters focus on the substance of American action. Chapter 5 deals with the Soviet-American struggle, and Chapter 6 considers a group of related issues. The list of recommended readings emphasizes books that exist in paperback format, as being likely to be purchased and made part of the citizen's library.

The author is indebted to his colleagues on the faculty of the School of International Service of The American University for their generosity and patience during the preparation of this book. Prof. Abdul Aziz Said, in particular, served cheerfully as a critical audience and as a source of improvements in content and style. Mr. Philip Burgess, the author's graduate assistant, performed many thankless tasks with efficiency and energy. Several dozen other students in the School of International Service also contributed—some of them unknowingly—to the final shape the book has assumed.

Finally, the author's wife, already familiar with the stresses of scholarly creation, has borne her peculiar burden of intrafamilial dysfunction with much more patience, sympathy, and aplomb than the author had any right to expect.

Errors and misjudgments, however, are inevitable in any book. For those in this volume the author—with such resignation and cheerfulness as he can muster—assumes full responsibility.

Charles O. Lerche, Jr.

Contents

INTERNATIONAL RELATIONS

Chapter 1

Today Americans live and move upon a world stage. The freedom, the prosperity, even the very survival of the nation depend in large measure upon whether or not the international problems facing the United States are brought to satisfactory solutions. World affairs have become of vital importance and disturbing intimacy to everyone.

We begin our examination of the major factors in the world challenge to the United States with an analysis of the international system within which the nation functions. Although Americans bring to world affairs their own characteristics, purposes, and techniques, they must nevertheless achieve their ends in an environment over which they can never exercise more than partial control. The procedures and patterns we call "international relations" constitute a primary limiting factor on American freedom of action; a full appreciation of both the dangers and the opportunities facing the United States must be founded upon an understanding of the nature of the world system.

THE INTERNATIONAL SYSTEM

By "the international system" we mean the assumptions and procedures that govern the relations between the nation-states of the world. Although not elaborately structured (we shall be looking at its organized segment in Chapter 2), the international political order, albeit dynamic, is surprisingly systematized. In spite of an external appearance of catch-as-catch-can, an inner logic and force permeate international relations.

THE WORLD COMMUNITY   The whole of mankind and the entire surface of the earth are divided into a limited number of independent units. These are called "states," or (more accurately) "nation-states." The states of the world deal with each other as collective entities; international relations exists among the somewhat more than 100 states which constitute the "world community."

International relations began in Europe, where modern states first appeared at the beginning of the sixteenth century. As European influence radiated outward, the international community expanded to include certain non-European states; as late as 1920, however, Europe was still the world's political center of gravity. During the past four decades a great increase in the number of states (the League of Nations, for example, never had more than 50 members whereas the United Nations today has more than 100) has transformed the international system. Today international relations is common to almost the entire human race.

THE NATION-STATE   The nation-state, as we have indicated, is the basic unit in international relations. Nation-states differ from one another in size, in wealth, in power, in form of government, in social and economic structure, and in cultural tradition. All the rich variety of which humanity is capable is sharply demonstrated in the different forms assumed by the institution of the state. Diversity among men and societies is one of the governing assumptions of international relations.

But however much states may differ in physical and organizational characteristics, they are alike in certain key manifestations that mark each as truly a state. All, in the first place, occupy a definite portion of the earth's surface which is of no stipulated size but which must have clear boundaries. Second, all consist of a body of people organized for political life. Third, all possess a government capable of maintaining internal order and of conducting international business. Finally, all are endowed with "sovereignty."

Sovereignty makes a state a state, at least for international purposes. The term has been defined in many ways, but we may regard it simply as that characteristic that enables a state to participate in international affairs as a full member of the system. It is partly a product of the political self-consciousness of a people, but in the last analysis it must be explicitly or tacitly conferred on the state by the other members of the system who accept it as a fellow. It carries a number of implications of status, among the most important of which are equality, independence of action, internal jurisdiction, and international responsibility for its actions.

In the modern world the most crucial aspect of sovereignty is political; the facts of interdependence and organization have undermined the juristic rationale of the concept. But a sovereign state—however clearly it may recognize and act upon its inequality in power, wealth, or prestige as compared with its associates—considers itself the equal of all comers in dignity, status, and intrinsic worth. The defense of this position is a first charge on the resources of any modern government. This is particularly true in the case of the many new states that have appeared in the world since 1945. To them statehood is a novel and uniquely precious thing; they are avid to exploit their new status to the full and are prone to demand a complete measure of deference to their sovereign rights.

THE NATURE OF INTERNATIONAL POLITICS   Since the state is a political organization and since states—through their governments—conduct international relations, it is not surprising that political considerations dominate the relations of states. "International politics" is a more accurate name for what goes on between states than is "international relations," and we ought to make clear the real stakes of the international political struggle.

The state, we may assume, exists to serve human purposes. Each state (and its government) is an instrument of the dominant elements in the society for fulfilling, or at least enhancing, certain values which they hold in high regard. The foreign policy of any state, therefore, is an attempt at the maximization of more or less widely shared values. Politics in the international arena—as anywhere else—is a struggle among men who hold competing values and who seek their ultimate or partial vindication.

There is, in other words, no real basis for arguing that the purposes of American foreign policy are in any way superior to those of any other state, *except that Americans feel they are*; this very value judgment, however, is an ample justification for all the effort expended by the government of the United States. The value-centered nature of international politics is another characteristic of the system; it adds a dimension of emotional fervor and diminishes the control of rationality in interstate relations.

THE KEY PHENOMENA

Certain key phenomena and the concepts that refer to them are indispensable to an understanding of international politics in the real world. Each of the concepts is widely used in popular discussion, but we shall attempt to define each of them as precisely as possible. Precision in language is critical in the analysis of international politics; the loose use of terms, as it is in any serious study, is a fatal blow to accuracy and insight. The definitions and discussions that follow are admittedly not the only possible ones, but each has proved useful in analysis and projection. We shall attempt to use them consistently throughout the examination that follows.

NATIONALISM As suggested above, the dominant political form today is the nation-state. This means that each of the world's political units encompasses a nation. Nation is a word of many meanings, but we shall use it simply to refer to a people who share an emotion called "nationalism." The latter is a supremely important factor in contemporary world affairs, as indeed it has been for nearly two centuries.

Nationalism is the feeling that binds a people into a unit for their common political purposes. It involves initially a dual sense of awareness within the group: first, the essential identity of each member with all the others with respect to certain common values; second, the fundamental differences between the group itself and all other national units, sufficient to make it separate and unique. Nationalism incarnates the mass-shared values that the group seeks to maximize; these, when translated into concrete enterprises by the officials of government, become the basis for the state's foreign policy.

Nationalist values are infinite in number, but they tend to cluster within certain near-standard categories. Independence, power, prestige, dominance, prosperity: these and others equally as familiar represent the nationalist preoccupations of most peoples. Nationalism usually engenders either of two types of action program: the first emphasizes *protection* of the value system against external threats; the second concentrates on the *promotion* and *extension* of the human and territorial area within which the nationalist creed is accepted. Of course, protection and promotion are concerns of any nationalism, but different nations develop varying priority relationships between positive and negative orientations.

Nationalism, in other words, is the vehicle of the value system the state is seeking to fulfill in international politics. Its role within a state is to bridge the gap between the people and their government; as long as the state's policy harmonizes with nationalist aspirations, officials can count on popular support. Conversely, a government runs serious risk of repudiation if it develops a policy along lines contrary to the urges of a sensitive nationalism.

NATIONAL INTEREST National interest (another term of notoriously imprecise content) refers to the concept of long-range purpose for which both people and government see themselves as acting in the world. It is thus more explicit than nationalism, yet not so bound to immediate events as is "policy" (another basic term we shall examine in a moment). It is the idea—or set of ideas—which serves figuratively as the gyrocompass to a government, keeping it steady and on course irrespective of what interruptions may come from external forces.

In spite of its nonspecific nature, a reasonably well-rationalized notion of national interest is necessary to the foreign policy of any state. Foreign policy consists of an unending series of decisions; if a state's relations with other states is to be any more than a meaningless jumble of *ad hoc* opportunistic moves, it must have some continuing basis for orienting its action. National interest holds foreign policy together by providing a continuing criterion of choice, determining the selection of one alternative course from among the several open to the government at any time. In spite of constant variation in circumstances, a state may achieve a high level of consistency in its foreign policy by constantly using the criterion of interest to govern its response to all variety of stimuli. In its terms past actions are justified and future moves projected.

POLICY   Once national interest is solidly in hand, a state moves to its satisfaction in the world of men and events. Applying the yardstick of interest to the situation in which it finds itself, it develops a set of "objectives": states of affairs favorable to its interest that it feels it can and should bring about. These, we should add, may call for either the protection of an already satisfactory situation or the modification of conditions in a desirable direction. Objectives must be as concrete as possible if their attainment is to be realistically sought, for the more precisely a goal is formulated the easier is the task of devising a strategy for its achievement.

Once an objective is established, a "policy decision" in the pure sense is made; that is, a course of action aimed at reaching the objective is decided upon and set in motion. Policy (the word refers both to the decision itself and to the implementing action undertaken) must of course be constantly evaluated, and here again national interest serves as the controlling criterion. If such a reexamination reveals that the policy in effect does not advance the national interest but instead is inimical to it, the policy is (or at any rate should be) immediately modified.

The word "policy" is also used to refer to the totality of a state's international actions; we speak, for example, of "American foreign policy." In one sense, of course, this is inaccurate, for a policy can be no more than a single course of action designed to reach a discrete objective. In broader terms, however, the consistency derived from adherence to a controlling notion of national interest creates enough inner harmony in foreign policy that we are justified in using some such collective term. In any case, usage is so strong that we cannot help but accept the dual use of the word and content ourselves with hoping that confusion can be avoided.

THE POWER OF STATES   A state cannot count on the legality, the justice, or the wisdom of its case as it attempts to serve its interest and accomplish its objectives. It must instead rely on its power. States are absolutely unequal in the power they can mobilize in support of their purposes; the equality of states postulated by the doctrine of sovereignty coexists with chronic inequality in state capacity to achieve goals.

"Power" is the measure of the ability of a state to have its own way; in operational terms, it is the capacity of a government, in a given situation, to have other states agree with it. The term has, as we shall see, distinct overtones of coercion, but it is by no means synonymous with "force." A state that can count on the voluntary consent of another is as well off as one that must coerce acquiescence; force and consent combine to create the effective power a state may use.

A state's power potential is the result of the interaction of a number of specific factors, both tangible and intangible. Among these are geography and natural resources, industrial production, military strength, the quality of its leadership, and popular morale. But these categories can do no more than hint at the real power position of a state in a concrete situation. In a particular context a state can use only a part of its absolute power; the nature of the problem, its other commitments, and its self-imposed limits on possible types of action all help inhibit its real freedom of choice. "Power politics"—the resolution of value conflicts by the application of factors of power—is indeed the rule in international relations, but international conflict is likely to be settled by only partial commitments of power. Frequently, indeed, the state with the greater overall potential has less available for use than does its smaller adversary; weak states paradoxically often have a larger measure of freedom of choice than do great powers.

Power is whatever a state can use to help it gain an objective. The usable forms of power, therefore, vary in terms of the objective sought and the operational conditions. No greater blunder can be made than a crude equation of power with military force. Arms are a real power factor only in a context in which they will help achieve the end, and are irrelevant and distracting in circumstances in which other forms of power are controlling.

CONFLICT AND ADJUSTMENT The contacts between states are not at all the result of sheer accident. In practice, states almost always deal with each other in a context determined to some major extent by deliberate policy decisions on each side.

These relations may run the gamut from intimate cooperation and collaboration at one extreme to all-out war at the other. As a normal rule of statecraft, however, policy makers allow for the possibility (or, to be accurate, the near certainty) of some measure of disagreement and conflict in their relations with all other states. Actually, it is almost mathematically certain that no two national policies will coincide.

Interstate conflict is therefore one of our key phenomena. Although it would be a mistake to assume that all international relations results from controversy, it is undeniable that the phenomenon of conflict has a peculiar importance. The very notion of "power" presupposes disagreement and dispute, and the entire apparatus of diplomacy and statesmanship makes ample provision for the promotion of national interest in a climate of controversy.

But, despite its centrality, conflict is only one side of the coin. Perpetual war—hot or cold—is an intolerable condition of human existence; a long struggle is acceptable only if objectives are won that justify the effort. As a result, the assumptions and techniques for adjusting disagreement and escaping from conflict are as crucial to the policy maker as those that pertain to the conduct of struggle.

Arranging tolerable solutions to individual disputes is a major responsibility of any working diplomat. His concern—in the usual case in which total satisfaction is impossible at a bearable cost and risk—is to develop a formula of settlement that is at least minimally acceptable to both parties as a basis for the liquidation of the conflict. Thus, most of the time conflict and adjustment go on within fairly narrow limits. Only when vital national interests are involved on both sides does dangerous crisis, defying routine adjustment, call basic issues of stability and survival into question. There is, in other words, a broad spectrum of conflict and an equally broad range of adjusting devices to deal with it. Prudent diplomacy usually seeks to place itself near the center of both continua.

STATE STRATEGY IN WORLD POLITICS

How does a state go about setting its course in world politics? What kinds of judgments must be made; what are the basic categories of decision? Although of course no two states answer these questions identically, the fundamental requirements of political life in the state system apply in the same general way to all governments.

SETTING GOALS AND OBJECTIVES The values that underlie all state action are postulated a priori. Each nation is the judge of the propriety of its own actions; others may or may not agree, but there is no universal criterion by which to judge. If these generalized values are to be useful as guides to action, however, they must be reformulated in sufficiently concrete and precise terms to permit their achievement. This is the province of goal setting.

A "goal" is usually thought of as a permanent or at least an enduring state of affairs, generally rooted in long-term environmental circumstances, to the accomplishment of which a state is prepared to devote itself. An "objective," by contrast, is the condition a state seeks to bring about within a single situational context. The United States, for example, may pursue the goal of hegemony in the Caribbean, while it may adopt the objective of eliminating a hostile regime in one of the Caribbean states. Goals are usually distinguished from objectives in terms of their longer analytical purview. Objectives, furthermore, are more susceptible than goals to amendment in the light of situational change.

Goals and objectives may be absolute (valuable in and of themselves) or intermediate (useful only as stepping stones to still other objectives). Most of the effort of states is in fact expended in the pursuit of intermediate objectives; diplomatic action usually consists of a series of small steps toward the ultimate purpose the state is serving. One unfortunate result of this concentration upon intermediate objectives is that often long-term purpose is lost sight of and arrangements and policies that are really only means to a larger end become transformed into self-justifying ends. The United States is particularly prone to this loss of perspective and its consequent diffusion of effort.

ANALYZING SITUATIONS Since all governments must conserve their human and material resources, they seek to act as efficiently as possible. This requires that the situation in which the state will act be analyzed as carefully and realistically as possible. Three different sets of factors must be evaluated and interwoven in order to develop a useful picture of the context of action.

The first relates to the international system itself. Historical forces that apply to all states simultaneously delimit much of the area of state activity. In a time in which change is rampant, for example, there is a much greater dynamism in international relations than during an era of stability. The state of technology, the vitality of international organization, the health of the world economy, and the intensity of nationalist identification are some of the other phenomena that contribute to the overall "climate of decision." All states are affected by the prevailing tone of international politics and must accommodate their decisions to it.

Second, all other states and their policies must be considered in some way. A policy maker must know what his opposite numbers have been and are doing about the problem, and what they will probably do in response to any action he might take. One of the most common reasons for action by a state is the need to respond to a move taken by one of its fellows, and an estimate of the reasons for the action and its probable consequences constitutes a large part of the situational analysis.

The final category involves the state's own capabilities for action. Independently of any preferences he may have, it is critical for the policy maker to know all the courses of action that are in fact open to him. At this point the abstract concept of power must be made concrete; here there is no question of what the state might be able to do in some hypothetical future confrontation, but rather what it can do within a given set of conditions. Most governments discover at this point that their real freedom of action is much more limited than casual judgment might have suggested.

When these three analyses have been completed, they are fused into an overall estimate of the situation. This is the evaluation upon which action decisions are based and in terms of which policies are framed and enterprises launched. In view of its centrality and importance, it is no wonder that a government normally places a high premium upon the accuracy and reliability of its evaluations. Miscalculation causes more failure in international relations than does stupidity or immorality, and miscalculation almost always takes the form of misreading the situation in which the state must act.

FACTORS GOVERNING POLICY DECISIONS   The objective established and the situation analyzed, the next step is the selection of a course of action. Normally the responsible officials develop all the open alternatives as fully as possible, attempting to forecast the consequences that would follow from the adoption of each of them. Measuring this set of expected outcomes by the controlling criterion of interest, the decision maker selects that one for implementation that promises the greatest advantage (or, as often happens, the least disadvantage).

The "cost-risk" calculation enters into the process at this point. Any action the state might take will cost something in treasure, effort, time, or even human life. The worth of the objective sought is the only justification for the effort, and ordinarily no policy is adopted that will cost more than the goal is worth. Some measure of risk is also involved in any policy move; the acceptability of risk is also determined by the relative and absolute importance of the goal. Determinations of cost and risk come most forcibly to public attention when the issue is one of war or peace, but they are a constant element in all decisions.

A variety of political judgments also affect policy decisions. No policy maker dare lightly violate the mass consensus upon which he relies for support and implementation. He may not ignore the wishes of his allies nor the expected reaction of neutral or hostile states. He must also allow for the possibility that opinion in his own government may not be unanimous about the extent to which the national interest is involved or the demands of the situation.

Policy making, therefore, is not a clear-cut process of choosing the most profitable alternative, but instead requires great flexibility and subtlety. Statesmen accordingly seek always to retain the maximum freedom of maneuver when making a decision. This concern ordinarily leads them in the first place to commit themselves only to the minimum necessary in the situation and in the second to leave themselves whenever possible a convenient avenue of retreat. State strategy is, above all, an exercise in prudence.

TECHNIQUES OF ACTION   An action decision calls for the application of the state's available power to the pursuit of the objective. Power in international relations may be employed in four different areas: the political, the economic, the psychological, and the military. Within each of these general categories, of course, an infinite number of specific steps can be taken. The choice of which technique (or, more commonly, which combination of techniques) to use is made by the responsible officials in terms of the objective sought and the opportunities and inhibitions intrinsic to the situation.

Political action, by means of the instrument of diplomacy, is a constant of interstate life. As a technique of policy its outstanding characteristic is directness: a government can by diplomatic means exert pressure explicitly upon the decision makers of other states. Although of great utility in situations of persuasion or compromise, diplomacy is limited in coercive effect; it gains greatly when it is used in conjunction with other techniques of power.

Economic action is a technique of great versatility. It may be either persuasive or coercive: a state may attempt either to enrich or impoverish another. It is, under appropriate conditions, exceptionally effective, but it suffers from one serious shortcoming. Economic power is often unpredictable in its direct results, and invites retaliation in kind from the state affected.

Psychological action is the province of propaganda and psychological warfare. Here the object is to create in the other state a climate of opinion favorable to the propagandist's purposes or at least incapable of resisting them. In spite of its contemporary popularity, psychological power is of limited direct effectiveness as a coercive tool; it does, however, lend greater emphasis to those political, economic, and military moves with which it is coupled. The new sophistication about psychological techniques is illustrated by the extent to which such devices as "cultural offensives" have replaced hostile propaganda in the contemporary world.

Military action is both the most obvious and the most final form of state power. Its purpose is to break the enemy's will to resist by the threat or the use of direct physical force. It has long been recognized that this form of power is the only one that can produce final solutions to international disputes, and international relations has long accommodated itself to its possibilities. Because of the greater cost and risk involved in military action, however, states have tended to rely on war only as a last resort. As the cost and risk of war have increased with the advancement of technology, moreover, the practical range of utility of armed action has sharply narrowed.

THE PROBLEM OF WAR

Of all the aspects of international relations, Americans are—for natural reasons—most interested in avoiding major war. Today war is so horrible, with the certainty of widespread death and destruction and the possibility of the obliteration of all life, that it exercises an almost morbid fascination. This is by no means a misplaced emphasis; war is indeed the major international problem of our age.

WAR IN THE INTERNATIONAL SYSTEM   The system of states is composed of political units that recognize no loyalty or obligation to anyone outside themselves. Sovereignty makes each state a free agent. There are no institutions to impose settlements on disputing states as there are to regulate private controversies. States must resolve their disagreements themselves.

The most frequent avenue of escape from conflict is a compromise that gives each party some gain to compensate for its effort. But compromise is a voluntary procedure; it cannot be effective unless both sides agree. When no mutually acceptable terms of settlement can be discovered, the controversy reaches the point when policy makers must decide whether to push their case further. At this point the only technique left open is war, or at least its threat.

War in the international order plays the indispensable role of providing solutions to what otherwise would be mutually frustrating stalemates. It makes political life possible on the basis of national sovereignty and has won many otherwise unattainable objectives for states. It is, in a word, neither a pathological accident nor an immoral and irrational exercise, but instead a central feature of the normal theory and practice of international politics.

THE BASES FOR ACCEPTING WAR A very careful cost-risk calculation, even more precise than the usual one, must precede a decision to employ war as a tool of policy. Miscalculation or ignorance is always detrimental to national action, but in a climate of war they may be fatal. National survival demands the utmost that a statesman can offer.

A state contemplating war must be absolutely certain that the objective it is seeking is worth what a successful war will cost. It dare not resolve doubtful judgments in its own favor; it must measure its goal against the highest price it can foresee itself paying for victory. Even after concluding that the objective is worth its probable cost, the state must discover if the odds in favor of victory are sufficiently attractive—both in terms of the probability of winning and of the penalty for defeat—to make the war a worthwhile investment. There is risk in any form of political action, but in view of the high stakes of war it is foolhardy to increase deliberately the burden of risk without compensation for the added danger.

We are, of course, discussing "rational" war—war adopted as a policy technique. Wars may also be irrational: begun without the preliminary calculations we have outlined. This type of war is often the most savage and bloody, but its most regrettable characteristic is its uselessness. War can be faced calmly only in pursuit of a valid national objective. To subject men to privation and death for frivolous reasons—or for no reasons at all—seems a near-criminal waste.

If the cost-risk calculation is thorough and realistic and produces an affirmative answer, the state is free to act. Often, if it makes its intention known to its prospective enemy, no actual combat will be required; the other state will have undertaken similar analyses and will have concluded that—within the terms of the dispute—surrender may be rationally preferable to hopeless resistance. If, however, the second state feels the objective is too important to concede or if it feels its chances of winning the trial by arms are sufficiently good, it will force the issue to the battlefield. Here the accuracy of the respective calculations receives its only valid test. Many a misapprehension has been brutally exposed in the course of war.

THE NEW WARFARE We have been considering the classic theory that violence is to be proportionate to the value of the objective sought. Strategy has long demanded that no more damage be done to the enemy than is absolutely necessary to win his surrender. During the years since World War I, however, this doctrine of graduated violence has been undermined by the new technology of warfare.

Modern weapons and delivery systems have escalated warfare to the point of absolute destruction. Today only total war is probable among major powers. Any armed conflict between nuclear states can be efficiently fought only totally: total in weapons, total in geographic scope, total in targets, and—most importantly—total in objectives. Any war thus becomes a war of annihilation; the objective no longer determines the level of violence but is itself determined by the very means of war.

The difficulty of harnessing total war to a comprehensible set of political objectives has given international politics since 1945 strong overtones of frustration. Few objectives beyond sheer survival are worth the cost of victory in a nuclear war; the price of defeat is so awful to comprehend that an enormous—and so far unattainable—margin of superiority is necessary before the risk becomes bearable. The perfection of the techniques of war has paradoxically almost destroyed its usefulness.

Various modifications in warfare have been attempted to break this dilemma. Considerable attention has been paid to the possibility of limited war—i.e., subnuclear combat for less-than-total objectives. In spite of the persuasiveness of this argument in the abstract, no statesman has dared to attempt such a war; a little war can grow into a large one with stunning speed. Guerrilla warfare, at the opposite pole from total war in its decentralization and irregular tactics, has proved to be of considerable value in specialized situations. But by its very localized nature, however, it can fill only a small part of the void left by total war. "War by proxy"—great-power support of one or both sides in a civil or guerrilla war—has not produced political gain to the great powers proportionate to its risks.

ALTERNATIVES TO WAR If war cannot play its historic role in international politics, states must develop other methods of meeting this need, if the international system is to endure. The first decade and a half after

World War II did not, unfortunately, advance the world very far toward this goal.

The most ambitious effort to develop alternatives to war has been made by the United Nations. In spite of some unquestionable successes, the United Nations has not yet found any method of reaching acceptable solutions to the crises of the cold-war era. The fault, of course, does not lie with the organization, but in the policies its members pursue.

Only when peoples and governments accept the narrower operational limitations on their foreign policies imposed by the erosion of military power can the discussion of "alternatives to war" become realistic. Unless some way of breaking the technological "balance of terror" can be discovered, however—and few scientists offer much encouragement in this effort—the day of such a reassessment cannot be delayed much longer.

Review Questions

1. What are the characteristics of the state? Why is state sovereignty so important to international relations?

2. Show the way in which nationalism affects the foreign policy of a state and the course of international politics.

3. Show the relationship among national interest, national objectives, and national policy.

4. What are the factors in the situational analysis a state makes before taking action?

5. What is the role of the cost-risk calculation?

6. Demonstrate the role played by war in the international system.

INTERNATIONAL ORGANIZATIONS

Chapter 2

Sovereignty presupposes a divided world, and international politics is founded upon the principle of diversity. Ever since the birth of state life, however, and increasingly in recent years, men have realized the desirability of minimizing and overcoming their divisions. As a result, a surprisingly large number of formal associations of states now exist, complete with specified powers and structural forms. These "international organizations" in the aggregate conduct a major and increasing share of the relations of states.

THE NATURE OF INTERNATIONAL ORGANIZATION

An international organization is a formalized grouping of a number of states brought together for the accomplishment of common purposes. In spite of great variation in detail, they spring from a single motivational source and display marked similarities in philosophy and organization.

Sovereignty, it is important to note, is religiously preserved. An international organization is by no means a supranational government. The institutional structure is no more than a mechanism for implementing a preexisting will to joint action. In being careful not to underestimate international organization, we must be equally scrupulous not to overestimate either its scope of effectiveness or its psychic base.

REASONS AND PURPOSES International organizations owe their existence to the invalidity of the basic premise of national sovereignty. In fact, interdependence rather than independence is the rule among nations; the nation-state is not self-sufficient nor is it capable of fulfilling the needs of its people. Only joint action can offer any promise of a solution to the basic issues of survival and well-being on the planet today.

Two disparate but related urges have led to the trend to organization. The first is the danger of war and the desire to discover some less fearsome method of solving international disputes. The second grows from the mushroom spread of modern technology that has spawned a host of problems beyond unilateral solution. One (or both) of these lies at the bottom of any international organization.

Broadly considered, the purposes of international organization are evident in what we have been saying. In the first instance, all—but especially what we can call "general" international organizations like the United Nations—have as a purpose the peaceful settlement of disputes and the restraint and/or punishment of those states who would use war as a tool of policy. The second great purpose of international organization is welfare as interpreted by the twentieth century; supranational problems of all nonpolitical sorts are attacked in the interest of the betterment of mankind generally. Thus, the two purposes of international organization are comparable to the "protection" and "welfare" categories into which the activities of domestic government are usually divided.

COMMON CHARACTERISTICS Although no two international organizations are alike, they all demonstrate certain general characteristics that identify the form. Each owes its existence to a basic charter or constitution that takes the form of a multilateral treaty among the members; the powers, structure, and procedure of the organization are spelled out in this document. Only the signatory states are "members"; individuals cannot "belong." All organizations provide for a central policy-making body, composed of delegates from all the members and meeting regularly; in this body each member has one vote, and the traditional rule of unanimity is only now beginning to be breached. Some form of administrative corps to execute the mission as spelled out by the central body is universal; this includes always a professional secretariat and occasionally a core group of members. The organizations are all financed by contributions from the membership; the amounts are determined on a rough scale of ability to pay.

DEVELOPMENTAL TRENDS During the hundred or more years international organizations have formed part of international life, certain developmental trends have been constant. All have become much more pronounced in recent years, and there is some reason to expect a rather fundamental transformation in the structure and process of international organization in the fairly near future.

The most obvious of these trends has been the steady and marked increase in the membership of all types of international organizations toward the goal of universality. The vast increase in the number of states in the world has led to an equivalent growth in the size of international bodies; the most important organizations today average around a hundred members.

Related to increased membership is an augmented prestige. Today almost all international organizations are accepted as "international persons" in at least a political—if not yet a legal—sense. Membership, especially in the United Nations, is prized as a badge of full political maturity, and very few withdrawals of members have taken place in recent years from all organizations.

A third trend is a steady increase in the scope of competence and authority. Traditionally, matters falling within the "domestic jurisdiction" of a member were held to be beyond the purview of an organization. Although the principle is still retained, the definition of domestic jurisdiction is steadily being reformulated—against the objections of many states—so as to bring more and more borderline cases into the range of the international body.

Fourth, a greater effectiveness has been obtained by the retreat from the rigid principle of unanimity in making decisions. Vetoes are becoming rare as the principle of majority rule becomes established; this means that a state faces the possibility of being bound without its expressed approval. In the League of Nations, for example, every member had a veto, but in the United Nations only five major states have this power.

Finally, there has been a clear trend toward increased technical competence in dealing with problems. The professional civil servant loyal to the organization's purposes has given these bodies dedicated and skilled staffs that perform their missions with speed and efficiency. In fact, the principal obstacle today to the formulation of clear policy within an international organization is more a result of the political bickering among its members than of the organization's own inability to solve its problems.

THE UNITED NATIONS SYSTEM

The best-known and the most elaborate international organization in the world today is the United Nations. A "general" or multipurpose grouping, both its symbolic importance and its real relevance to world affairs make it a unique critical force. As such it deserves serious and detailed study by anyone interested in America's future course.

The chart illustrates its general structure and the relationship among its parts. The United Nations is based on its Charter, drawn up at San Francisco in 1945. There are six "principal organs" that together perform its work. Membership today is over 100, and includes all the independent states of the world except a small number of victims of cold-war partition (Germany, Korea, and Vietnam, for example). In terms both of scope of interest and of broad participation, the United Nations approximates the often-imagined "Parliament of Man."

The six principal organs are the General Assembly, the Security Council, the Economic and Social Council, the Trusteeship Council, the International Court of Justice, and the Secretariat. Most of the activity of the United Nations takes place at its headquarters in New York, although of course the world is its true arena of action.

THE GENERAL ASSEMBLY The heart of the United Nations is the General Assembly. All members are represented; each state has one vote (although of course its delegation may be larger). The Assembly meets in regular session for several months beginning early each autumn, but special sessions may also be held. The Assembly elects its own president, usually a well-known representative of a small state.

The General Assembly does most of its work through its main committees on which all members hold seats: (1) Political and Security; (2) Economic and Financial; (3) Social, Humanitarian, and Cultural; (4) Trusteeship; (5) Administrative and Budgetary; (6) Legal. In addition, there is a Special Political Committee and numerous standing and *ad hoc* committees ranging in size from the full membership to one state or person.

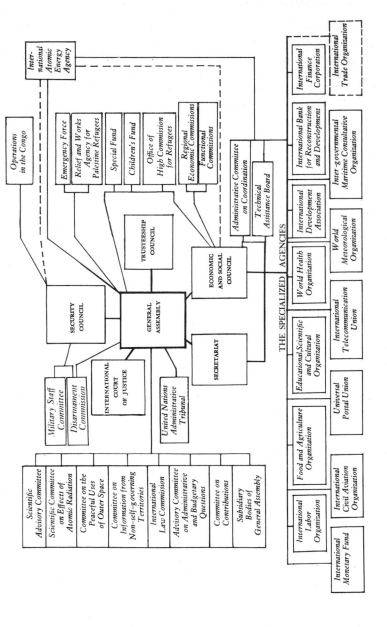

The United Nations and Related Agencies

Voting is by a majority of those "present and voting," except that on certain important questions a two-thirds vote is required. There is no veto in the General Assembly. The Assembly is competent to discuss any matter within the scope of the Charter and to make recommendations on any question except one under active consideration by the Security Council. Resolutions of the General Assembly, however, are not considered binding on members, but are very powerful nevertheless as the voice of mass opinion in the world. In recent years the General Assembly has become the most significant part of the United Nations on matters of maintaining peace and security.

THE SECURITY COUNCIL   The Security Council, a much smaller body than the General Assembly, has initial and primary jurisdiction over international disputes and other situations that threaten peace and security. It is empowered by the Charter to make recommendations for the pacific settlement of an international dispute (Chapter VI); it can also (under Chapter VII) act broadly—up to and including the use of the armed force of members—in case of a threat to the peace, a breach of the peace, or an "act of aggression." The peace-keeping activities of the United Nations are concentrated in the Security Council, and all members are bound by any decision it takes.

Keeping the peace is a task for major powers, and their special role is shown in the structure of the Security Council. Of its eleven members, five (the United States, the U.S.S.R., the United Kingdom, France, and China) are permanent. There are six nonpermanent members, chosen by the General Assembly for two-year terms with an eye to geographic and ideological distribution. Thus, the Security Council has its key members in a permanent status.

The privileged position of the permanent members is demonstrated in the voting arrangements. On "procedural" matters, an affirmative vote of seven members is necessary for action; on "all other matters"—substantive questions—the seven "yes" votes must include all five permanent members. This is the famous "veto": any permanent member may frustrate the other 10 by a "no" vote. What is more, the question of whether a matter is procedural or nonprocedural is itself nonprocedural and thus subject to veto by any permanent member.

The cold war destroyed great-power unanimity, and the Security Council has been largely paralyzed by the veto. The Soviet, of course, has been most free with its power to prevent action. The formidable grants of power given the Council by the Charter have remained largely dead letters, and the General Assembly has moved into the gap. There is, however, nothing wrong with the Security Council that a fresh infusion of great-power agreement could not cure; any relaxation in cold-war tension would see a great increase in the Council's effective role.

THE ECONOMIC AND SOCIAL COUNCIL   The Economic and Social Council is in reality a committee of the General Assembly, charged with implementing the "nonpolitical" responsibility of the larger body. The Assembly has broad competence in economic, social, cultural, educational, health, and related fields; the Economic and Social Council acts as a command center and clearinghouse in these areas and reports directly to the parent body.

The Council itself consists of 16 members chosen by the General Assembly for three-year terms, one-third retiring each year but immediately eligible for reelection. Membership tends to be representative of the various cultures represented in the organization. Voting is by majority with no veto. The Council directly supervises its economic and "functional" commissions (note chart) and certain special bodies such as the United Nations Children's Emergency Fund (UNICEF), and coordinates the work of the specialized agencies. Certain nongovernmental organizations have a "consultative" relationship with the Council as well.

THE TRUSTEESHIP COUNCIL   The United Nations has broad responsibilities for the welfare of "non-self-governing territories" in general, and of "trust territories" in particular. Article 73 of the Charter established the principle that all states ruling alien territories should have the welfare of the peoples as their primary concern. United Nations trust territories—ex-colonies of Germany, Italy, and Japan and certain territories voluntarily placed in trust to the United Nations—are under the particular scrutiny of the Trusteeship Council. This body is also especially interested in the implementation of Article 73, although the General Assembly has final control.

The Trusteeship Council has three classes of members: First, states administering trust territories (Australia, Belgium, France, Italy, New Zealand, the United Kingdom, and the United States); second, permanent members of the Security Council who do not have trust territories (the U.S.S.R., China); third, as many other (usually ex-colonial) states as are necessary to balance the membership equally between administering and nonadministering states. There is no veto, but due to the very explicit directives under which the Council works, votes are neither frequent nor important.

THE INTERNATIONAL COURT OF JUSTICE The International Court of Justice is the judicial arm of the United Nations. It consists of 15 judges representing the world's various legal systems, no two of whom may be nationals of the same state. They are elected for nine-year terms by the General Assembly and the Security Council voting independently, and are eligible for reelection.

The Court may hear only cases involving states, since individuals have no status before the Court. Its jurisdiction consists of those disputes which the parties agree to submit to it and certain categories that come to it automatically under the terms of the Charter or other treaties. Its judgments are binding on the parties and the Court has a good record of compliance. It may also, on request of another organ of the United Nations or a specialized agency, deliver an "advisory" opinion on a problem without any disputatious case. These latter opinions are very influential but are not legally binding.

In its work the Court applies the following categories of law: (1) "International conventions, whether general or particular. . . ."; (2) "international custom, as evidence of a general practice accepted as law"; (3) "the general principles of law recognized by civilized nations"; (4) "judicial decisions and the teachings of the most highly qualified publicists . . . as subsidiary means. . . ." The Court may also decide a case *ex aequo et bono* (according to equity and justice). Thus, the Court is truly a court of law.

THE SECRETARIAT The Secretariat, in spite of its name, is more than a mere collection of clerks and technicians, as it was in the League of Nations. It is a principal organ of the United Nations, and as such has its independent role and personality. The technical and administrative tasks are still performed, but upon these has been grafted a distinct political function. The Secretariat is by no means the least significant portion of the United Nations.

This is particularly obvious in the key role played by the Secretary-General himself, the "chief executive officer" of the United Nations. By no means self-effacing bureaucrats, the first three occupants of the post instead developed the office into one requiring real statesmanship. Something we might call a "United Nations presence" in world politics has appeared, finding its source in a generalized consensus among the smaller members and its expression in the intense diplomatic activity (and—as in the Suez Canal Zone and the Congo—occasional use of armed force) undertaken by the Secretary-General in the name of the United Nations. On several occasions he has been one of the absolutely critical three or four personalities to be involved in a major crisis.

He may, according to the Charter, "bring to the attention" of the Security Council any matter which *in his opinion* may threaten peace and security, and he makes an annual report to the General Assembly. These two powers give him an enormous role in the deliberations of the organization, and he has been anxious to play his part to the full.

The Secretariat staff is multinational and is made up of international civil servants, meaning that their responsibility is entirely to the United Nations itself. They are not to be tampered with by their respective governments in any way. They enjoy certain diplomatic privileges and immunities in the course of their work. Subsections of the Secretariat staff are assigned to the Economic and Social Council, the Trusteeship Council, and other organs as needed.

THE SPECIALIZED AGENCIES

Generally considered as parts of the "United Nations system," but actually full-fledged international organizations in their own right, are the several "specialized agencies." Each exists to expedite the performance of a single specialized international mission, usually of a technical and relatively nonpolitical character. In this respect their frame of reference is clearly distinguishable from the United Nations itself, which is multipurpose in structure and obviously political in orientation.

NATURE OF THE SPECIALIZED AGENCIES   Each of the 15 agencies (of which one has been dissolved and one has never come into existence) is a distinct international organization with its own constitution, budget, headquarters, and staff. Each state decides which specialized agencies it will join in terms of its own interests and needs. The Charter requires that the specialized agencies be "brought into relationship" with the United Nations; these arrangements provide for reporting and cooperation by the agency and coordination and Secretariat assistance by the central body working through the Economic and Social Council.

TYPES OF SPECIALIZED AGENCIES   The specialized agencies are of four functional types. The first group consists of those concerned with essentially technical matters of a high degree of mutual concern (ICAO, IAEA, IMCO, WMO, UPU, ITU). The second includes organizations of a primarily social and humanitarian purpose (ILO, UNESCO, WHO, and the dissolved IRO). The third is a homogeneous and closely integrated bloc of bodies designed to cope with international financial problems, especially those involving economic development (BANK, FUND, IFC, IDA). The fourth and smallest group deals with pure economic problems (FAO, the abortive ITO). Any new organizations that might be created will in all probability fall into one of the categories.

CHARACTERISTICS OF THE SPECIALIZED AGENCIES   The specialized agencies are remarkable in several respects. Their membership is surprisingly large; some (such as UPU) have many more members than does the United Nations itself. Their budgets, on the contrary, are exceptionally small, averaging only a few million dollars annually. The "central bureau" of each agency is the key element, being made up of a small group of highly trained specialists who work almost anonymously to carry on the mission of the organization. The assembly of each body is composed of government representatives, usually chosen with an eye to their competence in the work of the agency. The technical and financial agencies have reduced political interference with their work to a very low level, but the social and humanitarian bodies have been the battleground for many political and ideological issues.

PUBLIC INTERNATIONAL UNIONS

The specialized agency of the United Nations is the most advanced form of a very old type of international organization, the public international union. Born early in the nineteenth century, public international unions have flourished ever since, and today they are more numerous and effective than ever. Because of their highly specialized and often obscure functions, they are relatively little known. Their importance, however, is out of all proportion to their lack of renown.

ESSENTIAL CHARACTERISTICS   The public union—like its offspring, the specialized agency—is a single-purpose organization of states. Its mission is generally very technical and specialized, far narrower than that of the specialized agency. Its charter of incorporation is a treaty that lays down its scope and function explicitly. Its structure conforms to the general outline of an international organization that we noted above, but tends to the simplest possible framework. Its key element is its small but skilled professional staff—the "bureau" out of which the institution of an international secretariat evolved. The "conference"—an assembly of all members—makes policy, usually by unanimity, but meets only periodically. Public unions have proved to be remarkably stable organizations, and modifications in structure or function are rare.

WORK OF THE UNIONS There are several dozen international unions, each designed to perform a specific task. Their functions are generally classified into organizations for transportation, communication, scientific and cultural, economic, health, and social purposes.

The United States maintains membership in 33 public unions of various types, in addition to the United Nations and the specialized agencies. Eleven are pan-American in their orientation, such as the Inter-American Health Organization and the Pan-American Railway Congress Association. The remainder are general in their membership and include some of the most famous: the International Bureau for the Protection of Industrial Property, the International Bureau of Weights and Measures, the International Council of Scientific Unions, the International Hydrographic Bureau, and the International Criminal Police Commission (the famous INTERPOL).

REGIONAL ORGANIZATIONS

Regional organizations—a special type of international organization—today at least partially fill the gap between the United Nations on the one hand and the specialized agency or public international union on the other. A general international organization has a broad scope of competence and a heterogeneous membership; it is difficult in such a setting to generate sufficient consensus to furnish a base for action on issues of detail. A single-purpose agency, on the other hand, has ample agreement among its members but has only a narrow range of responsibility. Regional organizations, however, combine the broader concerns of the general organization with the more tightly knit membership of the special. In recent years the United States has exploited the utility of the regional approach to its international problems.

RATIONALE OF REGIONAL ORGANIZATIONS An organization may be "regional" in either of two senses. All its members may be physically located within a particular geographic area, or else its members—no matter where they may be located—share certain strong interests that cluster in a given region. By and large, contemporary usage leans to the latter meaning. The fact that most regional organizations consist largely of states that are neighbors only testifies to the obvious fact that they are all interested in what goes on in their own part of the world.

A regional organization is based upon a high degree of mutuality of interests among its members. It usually has a relatively small membership but a broad scope of action. If political in purpose, it tends to provide for a degree of policy coordination higher than found in any other organizational form; if economic, for the merging of economic policies and programs in stipulated areas by all members. Recently, the logic implicit in the idea of closely knit and broad-scope groups has begun to take overt effect, and several regional organizations have conferred broad grants of authority on their central agencies. There is, in other words, something of an evolution from mere alliances or associations toward the creation of real instruments of international government. In Western Europe, this has progressed to the point of actual transfer of some increments of sovereignty to the institutions of the European Community.

Most successful regional organizations today are examples of "functionalism" in action. The initial point of reference is the task to be performed, and structural and constitutional details are determined by operational requirements. There is no perceptible tendency today toward a standard form and procedure for regional organizations. Each —like the public international unions—is *sui generis*.

MILITARY-POLITICAL ORGANIZATIONS Most conspicuous among the various regional organizations are the military-political groupings that have flourished in the climate of the cold war. The United States has attempted to organize the major regions of the world into effective security systems against the danger of Communist expansion. In this effort the formalized regional organization has been a most valuable tool. On its part, the U.S.S.R. has organized its European satellites into a parallel arrangement, the Warsaw Pact (1955). Outside the direct cold-war orbit, the principal military-political grouping with a formal organization is the League of Arab States (1945), although the several informal blocs that have made their recent appearance in Asia and Africa may well develop in this direction.

The United States has gone farther than any other state in elaborating the military-political regional organization. The best known and most advanced of all is the North Atlantic Treaty Organization (NATO, 1949). This "keystone of American foreign policy" comprises 13 Western European states, Canada, and the United States. It provides a central headquarters with an international staff, regular meetings of foreign ministers for policy making, and an elaborate network of joint military arrangements under a single headquarters (Supreme Headquarters, Allied Powers in Europe—SHAPE). Its purpose is the joint defense of the territories of the members and the furthering of political and economic cooperation.

Similar in that they provide central institutions and machinery for consultation and joint action are the Organization of American States (OAS, 1951), the Southeast Asia Treaty Organization (SEATO, 1954), and the Australia–New Zealand–United States grouping (ANZUS, 1954). Although the United States is not officially a member, it participates actively in the work of the Central Treaty Organization (CENTO, 1959) for the defense of the Middle East. Thus, the United States has sought to ring the U.S.S.R. with regional organizations in Western Europe, the Middle East, Southeast Asia, and the Western Pacific, while protecting its own base in the Western Hemisphere.

Included within NATO is a purely European organization, Western European Union (WEU, 1955). This is a military alliance among Great Britain, France, West Germany, Belgium, the Netherlands, and Luxembourg. It cooperates intimately with NATO's military commands.

In recent years the NATO powers have attempted to develop a broader scope for the organization. One line of effort, led by the United States, has been to develop NATO into a distinct entity in world affairs by building up joint military strength, including nuclear weapons. France, on the other hand, has sought to weld the organization into a single bloc that will speak with one voice everywhere in the world. The smaller members, however, have instead sought to develop the as yet rudimentary possibilities of further economic and political cooperation with the eventual hope of creating an "Atlantic Community." Which of these courses NATO will take is still uncertain.

ECONOMIC ORGANIZATIONS The spontaneous development of regional economic organization has thus far been confined largely to Western Europe, although the matter is being seriously discussed within several natural groupings of young and underdeveloped states in Latin America, Africa, and Asia. The impressive list of accomplishments which the Europeans have to their credit has established a precedent from which perhaps the other nations of the world can draw.

Remarkable in the European experience has been the clear emphasis upon functionalism and the equally clear trend toward the creation of supranational authority. The story can be told as a series of steps.

The first move came in mid-1947 with the creation of the 16-nation Organization for European Economic Cooperation (OEEC) to coordinate the European end of the Marshall Plan. This set the pattern for intra-European joint action in the area of economic recovery and development. In early 1948, Belgium, the Netherlands, and Luxembourg formed a customs union which immediately became known as Benelux. In 1952, the European Coal and Steel Community (known as the "Schuman Plan" after the French foreign minister who proposed it) merged the coal, iron, and steel industries of France, West Germany, Italy, and Benelux into a single entity under a high authority possessing what amounted to sovereign powers. In 1958 the European Atomic Community (EURATOM) for the peaceful exploitation of atomic energy and the European Economic Community (the Common Market) for the development of a single customs union and common market were established among the same six nations. A single European community with some common organs for all three functional communities was created with headquarters at Strasbourg, France.

Spurred by the danger of being excluded from intra-European economic life, Great Britain moved to set up the European Free Trade Association (EFTA, 1960), which included—in addition to Britain—Denmark, Norway, Sweden, Portugal, Switzerland, and Austria. This group, also pledged to free trade among its members, came to be called the "Outer Seven" in contrast to the "Inner Six." Although there was some talk of a split in free Europe, both organizations were eager to develop a basis for cooperation and possible merger. In 1961, Britain, Denmark, and Norway applied for membership in the Common Market, while the three European neutrals (Sweden, Switzerland, and Austria) made application for "association" with the Market the next year. The failure of the negotiations in 1963 aimed at securing British membership was frustrating but by no means ended the effort to unite Europe.

It seems clear that the process of European regional development as it has evolved since 1945 has passed its embryonic stage. It will continue as an evolving factor on the European scene until it achieves fulfillment.

PROSPECTS FOR REGIONALISM   The prospects for regionalism vary with the type of organization and further depend upon the course of world relations during the next few decades. Some students condemn the entire regional concept and insist that virtually everything a regional organization can do can be better done by a perfected United Nations. To this argument one can reply that the United Nations is not perfect and that in regionalism many states have discovered a workable substitute for what the larger organization cannot do. Regional organizations, it would seem, have become a regular feature of the international scene.

The political-military organizations, particularly those to which the United States belongs, are largely creatures of the cold war. As such, their vitality—perhaps their very existence—depends to a great extent upon the future of the Soviet-American conflict. Were the cold war to dissipate, all would be affected and some would undoubtedly disappear. Only NATO seems likely to survive in any recognizable form, and then only if present trends continue to give it a broader base than that of pure military defense. The other blocs, however, are not likely to withstand the change in climate that would follow a major *détente*.

The present and future economic organizations, however, have really developed in response to more fundamental needs than those of the cold war and they would be very likely to grow even more rapidly if the inhibiting influence of great-power conflict were to be removed. Europe has in reality passed the point of no return, and its own dynamism is driving it toward closer and closer integration. The states of the non-Western world, responding to the urge for development and progress, will also be impelled to exploit some form of the same idea. In these terms regionalism obviously has bright prospects; its impact, furthermore, will ultimately be that of a stabilizing force in world affairs rather than a disintegrating one.

Review Questions

1. What is an international organization? What are the common characteristics of all international organizations?

2. What are the six principal organs of the United Nations?

3. Explain the operation of the veto in the Security Council.

4. Distinguish between the specialized agencies of the United Nations and other public international unions.

5. Characterize regional organizations with respect to the United Nations on the one hand and public international unions on the other.

6. Evaluate NATO as a regional organization.

7. Explain the steps in the evolution of the regional economic integration of Western Europe. Where does the matter stand today?

❖

HISTORY OF AMERICAN FOREIGN POLICY

Chapter 3

As these things are measured by historians, the United States does not have a very long record of participation in world affairs. America appeared on the international scene only in 1776, over a century after the birth of the state system. The United States is still feeling the consequences of its relatively late entry into international politics; Europeans (and many Americans as well) yet think of the United States as young and inexperienced in the conduct of foreign relations.

In spite of its relative brevity, however, the history of American foreign policy is well filled with both incident and interest. The history of America's international adventures merits serious study, and he who makes the effort will discover much that is both instructive and inspiring. Perhaps the most useful result of such an inquiry is an appreciation of the fact that—contrary to popular belief—the United States did not suddenly acquire a world role sometime between 1941 and 1947. Americans have in reality formed an integral part of the world community ever since they launched their first diplomatic ventures late in the eighteenth century. The dilemmas and difficulties of the present day to a surprising extent have their roots in the distant past.

American diplomatic history can be conveniently divided into four major periods. Before enumerating them, however, we should remind ourselves that history, divided into neat segments, is no more than a simple tool for the student. Things are never as orderly in reality as they may seem to be in a textbook. One era merges into the next by imperceptible degrees; the two may indeed overlap for a long time. The dates we shall be using to mark off one phase from another should not be taken literally, but rather as indicating important shifts of emphasis and direction in American policy.

Viewed in this light, the major periods of the history of American foreign policy are listed below. We shall devote one section of the chapter to each one:

1. The period of the discovery of national identity, beginning with the winning of independence and culminating at the end of the Civil War.

2. The period of the rise to great-power status, a process with its roots in mid-century but in fact largely compressed into a brief period around the beginning of the twentieth century.

3. The period of the "flight from destiny," covering the crowded years between 1914 and 1941, when Americans deliberately sought to turn their backs on the implications of being a great power.

4. The period of the full acceptance of national responsibility, beginning with the immediate prewar resolve to oppose the Axis dictators and continuing to the present.

THE DISCOVERY OF NATIONAL IDENTITY, 1776–1865

During the first half-century or more of its national existence, the United States had one major concern in foreign policy: the discovery and establishment of its distinctive national identity. Americans emerged from their struggle for independence convinced that they stood for something different—a conviction most Americans share today. The major international problem facing the United States was the translation of this idea into a set of workable policies.

THE BREAKAWAY FROM EUROPE   The United States owed its existence in 1783 to the workings of the international system it was joining. The Treaty of Paris that guaranteed American independence marked a truce in the long series of wars that convulsed Europe during most of the eighteenth century. France had been driven from America by the British in 1763; it took its revenge by helping the Americans shake off British rule two decades later. The United States, born as a pawn in the great-power game, immediately faced the danger of being caught up in a process with which it had no experience and over which it could exercise no control.

Alert to the risks, the leaders of the new nation set about neutralizing them. The task had two major goals. In the first place, if the United States were to be safe from great-power pressure it would have to eliminate the dangers represented by the remaining European footholds on the North American continent. Second, the United States could not afford to become a minor participant in great-power disputes; in practice this concern led to what later generations were to call isolation. The realization of these two purposes led to the establishment of a policy destined to endure for a century.

In seeking to guarantee the physical security of the nation, the American government drifted rapidly into a series of disputes with several great powers. The alliance of 1778 with France was repudiated and the United States refused to join in a new war against Britain; eventually French pressure led to an undeclared war against the United States. In 1812 the United States went to war with Great Britain for several reasons, not the least being an expansionist urge that called for the conquest and annexation of Canada. Spain as well felt American influence; her weak hold on Florida was menaced and finally broken by American infiltration. The infant United States proved to be notably belligerent in the maintenance of its independence.

The rupture of the French alliance was the first overt indication that the United States was to abstain from European involvements, but it only testified to an already deep-seated American preference. George Washington asked, "Why quit our own to stand on foreign ground?" and Thomas Jefferson warned Americans about "entangling alliances." Eighteenth-century Americans were determined not to follow Europe's course, but to seek one more in keeping with their unique genius.

In the end, however, the United States made good its escape from Europe only partly by its own efforts. The European system, in turmoil for a century, settled down after the Congress of Vienna in 1815, and great-power rivalries lost much of their sharpness. In the ensuing calm, the continued existence of the United States came to be assumed and its virtual secession from the system went almost unnoticed. By 1823, when the Monroe Doctrine signaled the complete independence of the United States from Europe, the danger had passed. The nation was launched on its self-determined course.

THE MONROE DOCTRINE   The first explicit formulation of the American position came in the Monroe Doctrine. The significance of these few paragraphs in President Monroe's annual message in 1823 was immediately recognized by both Americans and Europeans. It was a "second declaration of American independence." The lines of American policy were spelled out for all to read and ponder.

The Monroe Doctrine made three points. First, the United States declared the Western Hemisphere to be off limits to any future attempts at colonization by Europe. Second, the United States formally announced its indefinite abstention from intra-European politics. Europe was told to go its own way with no fear of American intervention. Third, the United States adopted a special posture toward Latin America as a natural area of long-term and major interest.

The first and last of these points are still very much alive and in fact form key elements in contemporary American policy. The United States has never abandoned its role as the protector of the Western Hemisphere against outside aggression, although modern defense arrangements are cooperative rather than unilateral. In like manner the United States retains its special interest in Latin America with heavy commercial, financial, political, and military commitments emphasizing its concern.

The second point—the repudiation of Europe—formed the doctrinal root of isolationism and affected the thinking of generations of Americans. European politics has long been felt to be only a trap for the United States that brings only woe in its train. After the United States attained great-power status, the demands of its new role clashed directly with the emotional biases of isolationism, and the tragicomedy of the twenties and thirties grew from this conflict. Even today, when isolation is buried as a base for actual policy, most Americans are still anxious about their "unnaturally" close relationship with Europe.

MANIFEST DESTINY   Turning away from the Old World was not merely an emotional outburst, but had a realistic policy basis as well. After independence Americans plunged immediately into the realization of their "manifest destiny." This initially involved filling in the continental hinterland of the original thirteen states, and was followed by the establishment of the principle of hemisphere hegemony and a breakout into the Pacific. All were accomplished by 1865.

Continental expansion proceeded in a series of great leaps, each accompanied by an international controversy. The first step—and the greatest in terms of territory acquired—was the purchase of the Louisiana Territory from Napoleon of France in 1803. By this move the area of the United States was more than doubled. Florida was then won from Spain in 1819. The Republic of Texas was annexed in 1845; the northwest corner was filled in by the compromise settlement of the Oregon dispute with Britain in 1846. In the latter year the United States had gone to war with Mexico. By the treaty of peace California and almost all the present Southwest were added. Only the Gadsden Purchase of 1853 was needed to bring the United States to its full continental expanse.

In the process of winning the continent, the United States had become involved with France over Louisiana, with Spain over Florida, with Mexico over Texas and California, and with Britain over Canada and Oregon. Three wars—the War of 1812, the Florida campaigns against Spain, and the Mexican War—and endless controversy accompanied national expansion. In the pursuit of manifest destiny the United States was willing to take on all comers.

Once at the Pacific, Americans did not hesitate but struck out across it. In 1844 the United States took the lead in opening China to Western penetration, although its interest was much more commercial (and missionary) than political. Of greater immediate note were the exploits of Commodore Matthew Perry of the United States Navy who in 1854 opened Japan to the outside world. American missionaries, traders, and planters were also making themselves at home in the Hawaiian archipelago. Americans did not feel that a vigorous and far-reaching policy in the Pacific contradicted their basic isolationist premise, even though great-power intrigue complicated their every move.

HEMISPHERE HEGEMONY   The unique place of Latin America in American thinking grew stronger during the middle decades of the nineteenth century. American trade penetrated the almost virgin markets of the young republics (early running into conflict with British interests). American filibusters and other adventurers found the unstable political climate congenial to their tastes and talents, several times embarrassing the authorities in Washington. Expansionists were already dreaming of Caribbean conquests, especially Cuba.

After the Mexican War, American statesmen began to think of an interoceanic canal in Central America that would shorten the sea route between the east and west coasts of North America by 8,000 miles. Official action to realize the project ran rapidly afoul of British influence in the area, and the final consummation of the enterprise was delayed until the twentieth century in large part because of the difficulty of reconciling the Anglo-American dispute. In actuality, of all the European powers Britain was the least willing to accept the restrictive implications of the Monroe Doctrine, and many Latin American disputes complicated relations between London and Washington.

The vindication of American hegemony at least in the northern half of the hemisphere came, however, at the expense of France. Emperor Napoleon III took advantage of America's preoccupation with its Civil War to set up a puppet empire in Mexico. Backed by French troops, this regime endured until the surrender of General Lee at Appomattox. The end of the war in the United States and a successful resistance movement in Mexico (led by Benito Juarez) hopelessly weakened France's position. Pressed by Washington, Napoleon beat a hasty and disorderly retreat. American supremacy was confirmed beyond any doubt.

THE CIVIL WAR   All Americans appreciate today that the Civil War is a landmark in their history, but not so many realize that it is prominent in the nation's international development as well. Although full great-power status was not granted the United States until after the Spanish-American War in 1898, the nation reached international maturity during the years of its internal strife.

Primarily responsible for this improvement in status was the massive military might mobilized on both sides during the war. Americans, distracted by the fury of the struggle and the gravity of the issues, failed to realize that they were fighting the greatest war in history. The other powers, however, were acutely aware that the United States—

so new to the international arena—nevertheless could field armies as large, as efficient, and as well-led as any state in the world. They were perfectly willing, on the evidence of the fighting, to grant the United States full membership in the inner circle of world leaders.

A second measure of the significance of the war was the way in which the United States dealt with several major international crises. We have already noted the strong line the United States took toward France during the Mexican affair. Also running through the war was a long dispute with Britain. London, tied economically as it was to the Confederacy, violated its neutrality by building several naval craft for the South. Washington became very blunt, going so far as to threaten war, and eventually Britain capitulated. In both these cases—and in others—the United States dealt with the great powers as a status equal, and was accepted as such by them.

THE RISE TO GREAT POWER, 1865–1914

Americans awoke only slowly to the meaning of their new status during the years between the end of the Civil War and the onset of World War I. Still isolationist in spirit and still certain they were "different," their international outlook never clarified. The necessary relationship between great power and large responsibility was missed until the very end of the period, the decade immediately preceding World War I. In that brief span the United States made an effort to rationalize policy with power and—as later events demonstrated—the general public did not enjoy the experience.

The history of the half-century portrays a deep conflict in the American soul between the consequences of power and the dangers of full membership in the group of world leaders. American foreign policy revealed this split. During these years it was a strange mixture of firmness and expansionism on the one hand and hesitancy and passivity on the other. The nation lunged into the future at breakneck speed but with constant nostalgic glances to the simpler past it was leaving behind.

EXPANSION INTO THE CARIBBEAN   Thanks to an already strong tradition, this schizoid tendency was escaped in one area: Latin America. Here no qualms inhibited the vigorous expansion of the United States. American influence flowed southward as earlier, and the task was made easier by the added prestige the nation enjoyed. Political manipulation of the republics of Central and South America was simple;

commercial penetration was equally untaxing. American nationalism found a safe and satisfying outlet in the Latin republics. So far did the American concept of "mission" go that in 1895 Secretary of State Olney could state flatly, "The United States is practically sovereign upon this continent, and its fiat is law upon the subjects to which it confines its interposition."

Especially significant was the first Pan-American Conference, held in 1889 at the invitation of the United States. From this first meeting of the American republics stemmed the Pan-American Union, the inter-American conference system that has endured to this day, the doctrine of hemisphere solidarity, and the Organization of American States (1951). It was also before this and similar audiences that the United States elaborated its self-assumed role of "big brother" and "protector" of the hemisphere—a position never popular with Latin Americans and, although never forgotten by the American people, eventually abandoned by their government.

Out of Latin American affairs also grew the most serious international crisis prior to the war with Spain: the Venezuelan boundary disputes of 1895 with Great Britain. The United States insisted on its right to decide a controversy between Britain and Venezuela, and took a high-handed line in pressing its case (Olney's arrogant statement was made during the crisis). Although Britain never openly conceded the principle, London eventually deferred to American wishes and accepted United States hegemony in Latin America.

The full flower of America's Caribbean policy was to appear only after the war with Spain, but its basic structure was laid down earlier. Protection, domination, and economic penetration were its ingredients; diplomatic and military pressure were its instruments. Americans have not yet been able to improve on this formula.

THE PACIFIC   After the Civil War the United States also kept edging further into Pacific affairs. Alaska was purchased from Russia in 1867. The benign relationship with Japan that dated from Perry's exploit of 1854 was maintained; during the second half of the century Japan was generally regarded as an American protégé. The United States also found its way into the South Seas, entering actively into the imperialist race into Samoa; in 1889 America joined Britain and Germany in a condominium over the islands.

The United States found itself most deeply involved in Hawaii. The rise of sugar planting in the island republic, largely by Americans who sold their product in the United States, brought Hawaii sharply to the attention of Americans. By treaties in 1875 and 1887 Hawaiian sugar received preferred entry into the United States; by the latter instrument Pearl Harbor was secured as an American naval base. During the 1890s expansionists at home and sugar planters in Hawaii launched a campaign aiming at annexation. In the midst of seriocomic intrigue, a treaty of annexation was drawn up only to be rejected by President Cleveland in 1893. A bitter controversy broke out in the United States, and Hawaii was finally annexed in 1898 only on the crest of a wave of patriotism engendered by Admiral Dewey's victory in Manila Bay.

THE WAR WITH SPAIN The Spanish-American War of 1898—a turning point in American history—was in its particulars a frivolous and unnecessary conflict, but in a larger historical sense it was all but inevitable. Americans had long been seeking to make their new power status more meaningful. In the brief and only partly glorious war with the decadent Spanish empire, the United States found an unmistakable symbol of its entry into full membership in the international order. When they added up the results of the war, Americans realized at last that the past had finally been left behind. The United States was now to make history instead of being only a spectator.

The war began with an attempt to liberate Cuba from Spanish oppression; it ended with Cuba only technically free but with the United States in possession of a globe-girdling empire. Puerto Rico and the Philippines were annexed, as were Guam and Wake Island; Cuba became an American protectorate. Thus, the United States (which during the war had also annexed Hawaii and half of Samoa) found itself a major Far Eastern power with its security frontier on the Asian littoral and also endowed with ideal Caribbean bases from which to project its power even deeper into Latin America. The United States had become an imperial state in a single bound.

The second great change brought about by the war was in American mass attitudes. The inheritance of a colonial empire triggered off a crisis of conscience within the general public, and a great debate raged over "imperialism." Events (notably an insurrection in the Philippines) helped the expansionists carry the field, and the United States headed into the twentieth century convinced that fate had chosen it for a major role in international affairs. Isolationism retained its emotional appeal but its political and strategic justification no longer existed.

THE NEW MONROE DOCTRINE   The new mission found its first expression in a reinterpreted Monroe Doctrine. The "corollaries" verbalized by President Theodore Roosevelt in 1905 and Senator Henry Cabot Lodge in 1912 claimed for the United States the right to regulate the internal affairs of Latin American states if these had international consequences. In 1903 President Roosevelt finally settled the issue of an interoceanic canal by obtaining a perpetual lease on a Canal Zone from the Republic of Panama after American influence had helped bring about that tiny nation's independence from Colombia. British approval of the principle of an exclusively American canal had been secured in 1901.

Also included under the umbrella of the Monroe Doctrine was what rapidly earned the derogatory name of "dollar diplomacy." The diplomatic weight of the United States was thrown behind American corporations seeking investment opportunities in Latin America. Once in a country, the corporation was assured of official assistance from Washington in its dealings with the host government. In spite of American arguments that this policy actually helped to civilize and modernize unstable societies, it created deep resentments among Latin Americans that survive intact to the present day.

THE OPEN DOOR   In its new role as a major Far Eastern power, the United States quickly found itself in a maze of political complications. Upset at the apparent intention of the major powers to carve up China, in 1900 the United States formulated the famous policy of the Open Door. This called for equal commercial opportunities for all foreign states in China and the preservation of that nation's "political and territorial integrity." These two principles were to undergird the American approach to China and the Far East until after World War II.

Its immediate consequence was the hostility of Japan. Recently come to maturity itself, Japan claimed a special interest in China and resisted American attempts to apply restraints. Japanese-American conflict, begun in 1900, reached its culmination 41 years later at Pearl Harbor.

THE UNITED STATES AMONG THE POWERS   Although the Open Door was the most obvious entry of the United States into major-power politics, during the first decade and a half of the century America gave every appearance of being in the game to stay. President Theodore Roosevelt accepted the challenge of history as he understood it and threw American influence into the thick of the struggle whenever opportunity offered. He personally expedited the settlement in 1905 of the Russo-Japanese War, he carried on a running dispute with Japan, he moved actively on Latin America, and he even "meddled" in European matters. It was a period without precedent in American history.

The other great powers—except, of course, for Japan—scarcely knew what to make of their new associate. Britain welcomed a possible ally, but no other state was happy about America's new role. France, Italy, and Russia found it difficult to take the United States seriously; Germany, although not seriously disturbed, saw in America a potential adversary. All of them watched, anxious to see what the United States would do.

THE FLIGHT FROM DESTINY, 1914–1939

In spite of the show of energy the United States had made after 1900, however, Americans were not ready to take their place in the world's political system. The outbreak of World War I touched off a reaction in the United States that endured for 25 years. For a quarter of a century America had only one major goal in its foreign policy: to insulate itself against the workings of the power system in the world. Only after complete failure had been unmistakably and repeatedly demonstrated was the United States ready to accept full responsibility in international affairs.

World war was a predictable outcome of the collapse of the nineteenth-century balance of power and, although cataclysmic, was in no sense abnormal. But to Americans it confirmed their worst suspicions about world politics, impressions dating from the birth of the nation and strengthened by over a century of provincial isolation. The old fears of diplomacy as only a primrose path to entrapment and impoverishment again dominated American thinking; isolationism—an admitted attempt to turn back the clock of history—formed the pattern of American response to the outside world.

WORLD WAR I AND THE UNITED STATES   The initial American reaction to the outbreak of the war was traditional: it was none of America's business. As the spreading conflict drew the nation closer to actual participation, however, two other ideas grew from the initial response: First, "those responsible" for starting the war should be punished; second, a system that made possible such a conflict should be destroyed and replaced by one that would allow decent men to live in peace and security. These two goals America carried into its actual conduct of the war.

American attitudes were fairly reflected in President Woodrow Wilson. An admitted enemy of "power politics," he became the self-appointed architect of revolution in world affairs. Democracy and peace were synonymous; he fought Germany both because it was aggressive and because it was autocratic. He passionately believed that a world order grounded on democracy, national self-determination, open diplomacy, the sovereignty of public opinion, and the League of Nations would be one in which peace and happiness would be the lot of all. In all of this he was expressing only well-accepted American political ideals.

To these ends he committed himself and his people. Neither he nor they ever fully appreciated how revolutionary the doctrine actually was, nor were they prepared for the brutally short shrift it received from the other victors. None of the Allies was ready for a Wilsonian peace in 1919—and, unfortunately, neither were Americans.

The crusading zeal of the United States was largely dissipated on the battlefields of France. When peace came, Americans wanted only to disentangle themselves, not to remake the world. Wilsonianism was largely repudiated at home even before the end of the fighting, and the President's position as a peacemaker was seriously compromised as a result. Disillusionment so great as to be only another form of illusion took command of the American mind.

THE REJECTION OF THE LEAGUE In the presidential election of 1920 "normalcy," in the person of President Warren G. Harding, won a great victory over Wilsonianism. The League of Nations was rejected and with it any hope that Americans would play a leading part in international relations. Neither power politics nor world reform had any appeal for the United States during the twenties. The prevailing tone was one of self-congratulation that America had so narrowly escaped being submerged in the treacherous waters of great-power politics.

By the twenties, however, true isolation had become an impossibility. Try as they might, Americans could not shut out the world completely. The United States, almost in spite of itself, was deeply involved in a number of major international problems during the decade. Among the more important of these were the following:

1. Disarmament. The United States took the lead in the movement for arms reduction, bringing about the first (and the only successful) disarmament conference at Washington in 1922 and participating actively in all subsequent efforts.

2. "War debts" and reparations. The interallied debts dating from the war and postwar periods and the related question of the amount and method of repayment of the reparations Germany owed the Allies kept the United States in the thick of European politics.

3. The Pacific. By the Four-Power Treaty and the Nine-Power Treaty of 1921 and 1922, the United States bound itself with the other major Pacific powers to recognize and guarantee the postwar *status quo* in the Far East.

4. The Pact of Paris. In 1928 the United States took the initiative in bringing into existence the Pact of Paris (known to Americans as the Kellogg-Briand Treaty), whereby ultimately virtually every state in the world solemnly renounced war "as an instrument of national policy."

5. Latin America. Dollar diplomacy reached its peak, with American military intervention into Haiti, Santo Domingo, and Nicaragua continuing to demonstrate American dominance. By the end of the twenties, however, the whole Latin American position of the United States was being reconsidered and the way paved for the inception of the Good Neighbor policy of the thirties and later.

Thus the twenties were not a period of total withdrawal. The United States was actually in the thick of important events much of the time. In two important ways, though, American policy was genuinely isolationist. First, American action was consistently unilateral and religiously avoided any cooperative or institutionalized permanent arrangements. Second, even the more forceful steps the nation took—such as disarmament or the Kellogg Pact—had disentanglement and isolation as their aim, rather than a more intimate articulation with the prevailing international order. Thus, in a strange and almost unrecognizable way, the Wilsonian dream of transforming international relationships retained its influence on American policy.

THE DEPRESSION   The Great Depression of 1929 accentuated these trends. With the League of Nations collapsing under the impact of Japanese aggression in 1931, the question of the war debts resulting in nothing but bad feelings on both sides, the European democracies floundering while the new dictatorships demonstrated frightening efficiency, and the

American economy grinding almost to a standstill, it is not remarkable that Americans turned their backs on the world. The thirties were as thoroughly isolationist as the United States could make them.

The only major break in this pattern occurred early in the decade on the occasion of Japan's aggression in Manchuria. In 1932, the United States sought vainly to gain multilateral support for its Stimson Doctrine of the nonrecognition of territorial change brought about in violation of treaty provisions. The other great powers refused to join in, and the United States, again disillusioned, set about trying to cope with the menace of Japan by itself. In later years, when similar crises reversed the situation, America was no more willing to act in concert than had been Britain and France in 1932.

THE ISOLATIONISM OF THE NEW DEAL   The New Deal era of Franklin D. Roosevelt added a new dimension to the American attitude. The New Deal was in the grand tradition of American reform; it subscribed enthusiastically to the primacy of domestic concerns and relegated foreign affairs to a distinctly subordinate place. Isolationism to the true New Dealer was both a historic policy and a profound ideological conviction.

This was particularly obvious in the economic sphere. Almost the first international act of the new administration in 1933 was a declaration of economic nationalism that wrecked the World Economic Conference. Although the Reciprocal Trade Agreements program, launched in 1934, aimed at the gradual reduction of tariffs, the New Deal insisted up to 1940–1941 that recovery at home took precedence over any projects for international economic improvement.

In more purely political fields the Roosevelt administrations of the thirties showed their isolationist bent. The decade was one of great international tension as first one dictator and then another made his move against the reeling democracies of the West. Neither in the case of Italy's rape of Ethiopia in 1935 nor in the open intervention of the Axis in the Spanish Civil War of 1936–1939 did the New Deal show any particular concern or even full appreciation of the danger. There was some sincere regret that these disturbing events were keeping the world unsettled but no disposition to take any action, either unilaterally or together with the beleaguered democracies.

Instead, the New Deal's recipe for coping with international crisis was the enactment between 1935 and 1937 of the so-called Neutrality Acts. These forbade Americans to sell arms to belligerents or to either side of a civil war. They were a reflection of the quaint notion—very popular during the thirties—that the United States had been lured into World War I by the "merchants of death"—the munitions manufacturers. The laws, still on the books when World War II broke out, were a perfect example of the American theory that danger could be shut out and the United States left safe in a world in flames.

In one area, however, the New Deal moved powerfully and to some purpose. The reevaluation of the Monroe Doctrine was completed. Dollar diplomacy was repudiated and replaced by the policy of the Good Neighbor and hemisphere solidarity. Military intervention was renounced as an American right, the protectorates of the United States were abandoned, and inter-American consultation on joint problems was declared to be the only action technique the United States would employ. The new solidity of the hemisphere and the vitality of the inter-American system proved very welcome when its help was needed during the course of World War II.

THE ACCEPTANCE OF RESPONSIBILITY, 1939–

The events preceding American entry into World War II brought the United States again face to face with history, and this time the nation met the challenge directly. The flight from destiny ended with the fall of France and the Battle of Britain in 1940. From that date Americans, however much they may be divided on details, have fully accepted the principle that the fate of the United States is bound up with that of the world at large. America is no longer an island unto itself, but a permanent part of the main. This drastic reorientation has simultaneously simplified and complicated the foreign-policy problem of the United States.

The years since the beginning of World War II may fairly be called the era of the acceptance of responsibility. Since 1939–1940 the United States has been seeking to discover its international obligations and to develop a policy adequate to their requirements. In playing a leading role in the conduct of the war, in actively planning for the peace, and in being a major actor in the drama of the cold war, the United States has been at last a great power in thought and deed.

THE RISE OF THE DICTATORS By 1936, the new Axis of Nazi Germany, Fascist Italy, and imperial Japan was in full stride, shaking the world with its daring and uniformly successful strokes. Britain and France, politically flaccid and economically stricken, could offer no resistance;

the U.S.S.R. was neither strong nor respectable enough to add strength to any anti-Axis coalition. The United States watched inefficaciously as the dictators struck in Manchuria, in Ethiopia, in Spain, and in the heart of Europe itself.

The United States was most deeply involved with Japan. In 1937 Nippon launched its invasion of China and ran immediately afoul of American objections. Incidents multiplied rapidly, and Japanese-American relations grew critical. As part of the slowly evolving American perception of the danger, in 1937 President Roosevelt called for a "quarantine" of aggressor nations and immediately launched a program of naval rearmament. But there was still no sense of real crisis; the passage of the Neutrality Acts and the inept American performance during the Spanish Civil War testified to an imperfect understanding of the situation.

The Munich crisis in 1938 precipitated some stronger American reaction toward the preservation of peace, although the nation was sharply divided over the utility of any "appeasement" of dictators. The Polish crisis of 1939 that brought on the war spurred the President to suggest mediation of the dispute, but even the diplomatic bombshell of the Nazi-Soviet Pact did not elicit any strong American response. The United States issued a routine proclamation of neutrality once the war began and set back to watch Britain and France dispose of the upstart dictators with little thought of the extent to which its own fate was involved in the struggle.

The fall of France and the Nazi conquest of Europe shattered this dream. In a few short weeks during the summer of 1940 America came to appreciate that its own safety depended on the frustration of Hitler and the survival of Britain. During the latter half of 1940 and almost all of 1941, a great public debate raged in the United States, in which the advocates of American action to aid Britain (and, after the Nazi attack in June, 1941, the U.S.S.R. as well) were slowly winning the battle. Government policy kept pace with the shift in public opinion, as President Roosevelt moved to make the United States an "arsenal of democracy" and to aid the Allies "by all means short of war."

The United States introduced conscription in 1940, traded destroyers to Britain for naval bases, convoyed war materials across the Atlantic, trained British aviators, and (in August, 1941) signed a joint declaration of "peace aims" with the British government—the famous Atlantic Charter. In the meantime, relations with Japan were growing steadily worse as Tokyo moved into southeast Asia in the wake of the fall of France.

Japan finally brought the crisis to a head with its attack on Pearl Harbor in December, 1941.

THE UNITED STATES AND WORLD WAR II   The United States fought its second world war very differently from its first. Almost immediately after becoming an active belligerent, the United States took the lead in forming the United Nations Organization. This grand alliance, ultimately including the 46 states at war with the Axis, pledged itself to a joint prosecution of the war and a joint peace. President Roosevelt, Prime Minister Winston Churchill of Great Britain, and Premier Stalin of the Soviet Union met several times during the war to frame strategy and decide priorities.

Also different from 1917 was the proportional share of the economic and military burden of the war borne by the United States. Its economic contribution to victory was by far the greatest of all the Allies, as floods of war production poured from American factories for the use of all. Its military effort was the most far-flung, involving major wars both in Europe and in the Pacific; along with the geographically more concentrated forces of the Soviet Union, it was the major architect of the eventual battlefield victory. There was no reluctant or half-hearted American participation this time; leadership descended on the United States almost without asking and the nation seized the opportunity.

PLANNING FOR THE PEACE   The United States—thanks to the Atlantic Charter—had begun planning for peace even before it became a belligerent. Lamentably, the substance of America's peace aims contained little that was novel or imaginative. The Atlantic Charter and all later formulations were all evocations of Wilsonianism as modified by the ideology of the New Deal. The "four freedoms" of Franklin D. Roosevelt blended nicely with the "fourteen points" of Wilson: self-determination, free trade, a higher standard of living ("freedom from want"), freedom of the seas, disarmament, and international security. From these principles America had never departed.

In more immediate terms, however, the United States recognized the inevitability of postwar spheres of influence and other aspects of pure power relationships. So far had America come since 1919. Less defense can be offered, however, for the political unsophistication demonstrated in the American insistence upon the "unconditional surrender" of the Axis. This "policy" worked reasonably well in the cases of Japan and Italy (which surrendered more or less intact), but led to disastrous results in Germany where the Nazis held out until virtually the entire political, economic, and social fabric of the state had disintegrated. Surrender left a total vacuum, and the seeds of the cold war were sown in the rubble of defeated Germany.

The high point of American planning, however, was the United Nations. This postwar organization was to be Wilson's final vindication. Americans insisted that this time the organization would work because the United States would take part from the very beginning. History, it seemed, was giving the nation a second chance, and the people were all the more anxious to participate because they were so conscious of having failed a generation earlier.

The American government took no chances of being caught off guard. Early in 1943 an interallied commitment to a postwar international organization was made official. The outlines of the Charter were worked on throughout 1943 and 1944. The troublesome points were settled at the Yalta Conference in early 1945. The San Francisco Conference to draft the Charter convened in April, 1945—even before Germany's surrender.

The United States felt, as the war ended, that it had rectified its two great historical errors: First, it had buried isolationism for all time; second, by joining the United Nations (indeed, by being the very first state to ratify the Charter) it had finally destroyed the system of power politics, aggression, and war against which it had been struggling for so long. Many essential points were missed, however. Americans did not understand that isolationism could be left behind only by accepting full membership in a power-political system or that utopia—in or out of the United Nations—was not to be had in an imperfect world. These shortcomings were to plague the nation in later years.

THE UNITED STATES IN THE POSTWAR ERA   Other chapters will consider specific elements in the history of American foreign policy since 1945. Here, at the end of our overview of the historical record, however, we should glance quickly at America in the postwar era with relation to its historical past.

In one major respect, since 1945, the United States has completed its great transition: it is a full and leading member of the international political system. American foreign policy is now part of the main current of history. What the United States does is of consuming and vital importance to everyone in the world. Through all the tense years since 1945, in spite of many reversals in American thinking, there has been no serious consideration given to any new attempt at withdrawal.

The new level of participation of the United States shows up most clearly in three ways. First, the United States has been the leader of one of the two camps in the most important single political phenomenon in the contemporary world, the cold war. Second, the United States has been a leader in the United Nations where the world's troubles have come increasingly to be deposited. Third, the United States has begun to learn how to act as a great power in dealing with the vastly increased number of small states in the world, a task of unsuspected complexity whose ingredients the nation is still learning.

In another sense, though, America has not yet committed itself fully to the implications of its role. The national distaste for international political maneuvering is obvious; the temptation to seek to "solve" problems, "punish" enemies, and "reform" the international order is always strong and sometimes irresistible. The illusion of a perfect victory that will release the nation forever from tension, crisis, and continuing responsibility underlies too much American policy. It will require a fuller measure of time before Americans accept the future merger of their destinies with the larger fate of mankind.

Review Questions

1. Characterize American foreign policy in each of the four periods into which this chapter is divided.

2. Show the historic phases in United States Latin American policy.

3. Show the historic phases in United States Pacific policy.

4. Contrast the policy of the United States toward the League of Nations with that adopted toward the United Nations.

5. Evaluate the impact of Wilsonianism on United States policy during and after World War II.

6. How "isolationist" was United States foreign policy from 1919 to 1939? Is isolationism a factor in United States policy today?

CONDUCT OF FOREIGN AFFAIRS

Chapter 4

The formulation and execution of foreign policy is the most important and the most expensive undertaking of the United States government today—if by "foreign policy" we mean all the incredibly varied activities that stem from the necessity of guaranteeing American survival in a disturbed world. It was not always so; for a century and a half the twin tasks of diplomacy and defense were carried on by relatively small and non-prestigious government departments. Since 1945, however, international affairs have invaded the remotest recesses of the government hierarchy, and virtually no aspect of national policy is without its important and frequently controlling international implications.

In this chapter we shall examine the organization of the American government for foreign affairs. We can, of course, do no more than hint at the complexity and elaborateness of the decision-making and administrative machinery; our major purpose will be to locate the important centers of authority, to indicate generally how they function, and to sketch the relationships among them. Our discussion will conclude with a brief word about the forms of American representation overseas.

THE PRESIDENT AND FOREIGN POLICY

Both by law and by necessity, the President of the United States (whoever he may be at the moment) is the key figure in the conduct of American foreign policy. In large part this is because the total responsibility is his: every foreign-policy move of the United States is made in his name. International practice requires that relations be conducted among the several "heads of state": those human beings who have the right and the power to speak for their respective governments and peoples. This lonely eminence is the President's alone. He cannot delegate away his responsibility, however much he may vest his subordinates with increments of his power.

It is useful to conceive of the President as being at the center of a web of governmental machinery. He controls its action, picks and chooses from the resources available to him, and may enter directly into the process whenever and to the extent he wishes. Different Presidents may structure their own roles to suit their personalities, but none can reduce or eliminate the importance of his role.

THE PRESIDENT AS LEADER   Ever since 1789 the office of the President has expanded both absolutely and relatively. Although of quite recent vintage, the President's function as national leader is never more critical than when he is articulating foreign policy. The public, the Congress, and the opposition party may dispute the President's leadership on any or all domestic issues; when he speaks for the nation to foreign powers, however, especially in a time of real or fancied crisis, he may confidently assume a preexisting consensus in his support. Americans expect their President to be an active leader in foreign policy.

Thus, the President is armed with a clear mandate from his constituents to exercise vigor and initiative in international relations. He possesses a limited number of important foreign-affairs powers under the Constitution, such as the authority to appoint ambassadors, to make treaties, to receive foreign ambassadors, and to act as Commander in

Chief of the armed forces of the United States. Congressional legislation has in addition loaded him down with literally thousands of detailed grants of power. In the last analysis, however, presidential foreign-affairs leadership is a function of the realities of world affairs and the prevailing image of the office in the twentieth century.

Presidential leadership is exercised in several ways. He has the mission of establishing a general line, translating mass attitudes and opinions into realistic objectives and workable policies. He is the principal guardian of public morale, communicating with the people and establishing the emotional and political climate in which decisions are to be made. He determines the level of intensity with which American policy is to be prosecuted. He seeks public support for new ventures that otherwise would risk repudiation. In sum, he acts as the intermediary between an imperfectly informed and often bemused public on the one hand and a rapidly changing and menacing world on the other.

THE PRESIDENT AS DECISION MAKER   As the Chief Executive of the nation, ultimately responsible for all foreign policy, the President inescapably plays a major role as the highest-ranking decision maker. He usually finds it most economical of his time and most conducive to good administration to confine his attention to issues of only the broadest import. He thus establishes a framework of precedents and directives within which his subordinates may work out detailed implementation. This is indeed the normal way an executive operates.

But foreign policy only rarely remains a routine task. Many detailed problems find their way to the President's desk. Probably the two most common types are (1) the jurisdictional conflict within his staff, which no one but he can finally resolve, and (2) the sudden crisis of such magnitude that only he dares make the decision because only he can assume the risk.

We should also remember that the President is free to intervene into the decisional process at any time and at any point he wishes to. He may involve himself in an issue at the level of great detail, virtually superseding the "desk officer" in the Department of State who would otherwise take action. He may rely heavily on the information and recommendations that flow from his subordinates; he may, on the other hand, prefer to be guided by his political instincts, the advice of other governments, his personal friends, or his own intuition. Each occupant of the office fills his decision-making role according to his own inclination, although in recent years there has been a clear trend toward its overall magnification.

THE PRESIDENT AS ADMINISTRATOR   The other side of the coin of decision making is, of course, the implementation of policy. A great share of the President's foreign-policy effort is expended in administration. He supervises the many officials who share the burden of staffing, coordinating, directing, and evaluating dozens of offices. He has many specific duties that owe their existence to legislative enactment. He administers many programs—of which foreign aid is a prime example —that obligate him to perform countless routine administrative tasks. Indeed, so manifold and complicated are the President's responsibilities in this field that the office is in a state of constant reorganization in an effort to reduce his operating span to a manageable size. The speed with which new problems arise to replace those solved, however, is not a hopeful sign. The President has not yet been able to escape from the administrative demands of his office so as to have more time for policy making.

THE PRESIDENT AND HIS STAFF   To provide the assistance he needs, the President has developed an elaborate foreign-affairs staff. We can do no more than list its more important components; certain parts are discussed further below.

Most of the staff is included within the administrative unit called the Executive Office of the President. At its heart is the White House Office, where the President's personal advisers and assistants are found. Other units within the Executive Office include the National Security Council (the President's top-level advisory body on security policy), the Council of Economic Advisers, the Bureau of the Budget, and certain others.

Also to be included in the foreign-affairs staff are certain key department heads: State, Defense, Treasury, and probably Commerce and Agriculture as well. The Joint Chiefs of Staff, through their Chairman, give the President military advice; the Director of the Central Intelligence Agency reports (through the National Security Council) to the President; the Director of the National Aeronautics and Space Agency advises the President on the important issue of space exploration. Add to these the many individuals who may be from time to time added to the President's circle of advisers on particular problems, and at least the rough outline of the extent of presidential assistance becomes clearer.

THE DEPARTMENT OF STATE

The core of the foreign-policy apparatus of the United States government is the Department of State. It is the one agency specifically charged with foreign *policy;* the Secretary of State is the senior foreign-affairs specialist in the executive branch. The Department has a hand in almost all policy decisions and makes many of them itself. Upon it is placed the heaviest single responsibility for the international relations of the United States.

THE SECRETARY OF STATE   The Secretary of State is still generally regarded as the "senior" member of the President's Cabinet. Today, however, this preeminence is less due to social prestige than to the importance of his tasks. He is legally the principal adviser to the President on foreign policy and is expected to provide guidance to all executive officers in international matters. This is obviously a crucial role.

In general, we may group his functions under three heads. (1) He is the chief adviser to the President. (2) He is the chief administrator of the far-flung activities of the Department itself. (3) He is a most important policy maker in his own right, dealing with the questions that fall to him as the result of his relations with the President and the workings of his Department. He must, because of the peculiarities of his position, usually carry on all three tasks simultaneously.

The President, as we have noted, is directly responsible for all international action taken in the name of the United States. This makes his relationship with his Secretary of State crucial. This relationship is remarkable for its elasticity, and its dimensions are established generally by the President's own conception of his role and the personal rapport between the men. One President may become his own foreign minister and relegate the Secretary to an inconsequential place; another may turn the entire problem over to the Secretary and confine his attention to domestic affairs. Examples of both may be found, but most Presidents have fallen between the extremes.

DEPARTMENTAL ORGANIZATION   The Department is organized along familiar pyramidal lines, and major subdivisions reflect functional differentiation. How the Department conceives its mission is clearly indicated by the chart on page 56.

THE GEOGRAPHIC DESKS   The busiest operating units within the Department, however, are subsections of the geographic bureaus and do not appear on the chart. A "bureau," headed by an Assistant Secretary of State, encompasses one major area of the world. Within the bureau (Far Eastern Affairs, for example) a further subdivision occurs into

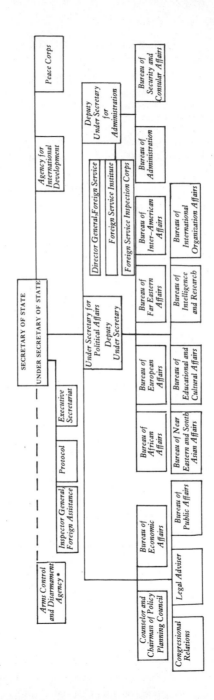

The Department of State. (From Manual of Organization, Department of State, January 17, 1962.)

*A separate agency with the director reporting directly to the Secretary and serving as principal adviser to the Secretary and the President on arms control and disarmament "offices" responsible for parts of the region (the Office of Southeast Asian Affairs is found within the Bureau of Far Eastern Affairs). Each office in turn is broken down into "country desks," with an "officer in charge" of United States relations with a particular country (a "Thailand desk" is in the Office of Southeast Asian Affairs). Large countries may demand two or more desk officers, while two or more less important nations may be combined within a single desk. These allocations of responsibility change to some extent in response to developments in American policy.

The desk officers carry a very heavy load. They are the principal avenue of communication between the Department and overseas installations, they deal with foreign diplomatic missions in the United States, they advise their several layers of superiors on matters concerning their desks, they make a great many policy decisions themselves. In many cases the state of American relations with a country is for practical purposes substantially in charge of the desk officer. Always his expertise is in great demand as a decision affecting his country is being made. The level of excellence of the Department can be no higher than that of its most important operating personnel.

THE FUNCTIONAL BUREAUS   The "functional bureaus" form an interesting part of the Department. Organized by function rather than geographically and not supposed to engage in operations, theirs is a staff responsibility: to aid the operating units (the Secretary and the geographic bureaus) by information and recommendations. To this general mission have been added a number of operational missions, however, usually of a specialized and nonpolitical nature.

The rich variety of the tasks the Department performs is suggested by the titles of the functional bureaus. Each was created to fill a specific need and each exists only as long as the need requires. Among the most recently created are the Chairman of the Policy Planning Council (elevated from the position of Chief of a Policy Planning "Staff") and the Assistant Secretary for Educational and Cultural Affairs. Others, such as the Legal Adviser, have a much longer history. In the aggregate the functional bureaus are responsible for a very large share of the Department's work load.

POLICY PLANNING   A vital part of the conduct of an effective foreign policy in the contemporary world is advance planning. The United States came to this realization only after 1946, but since then policy planning has had a permanent place in the Department of State.

The policy planners are supposed to be free of day-to-day operational responsibilities and to deal with a much longer time span. Their aim is to devise policies for the nation that will capitalize upon long-term trends in world affairs. Thus, the United States will be less likely to be surprised by unanticipated turns of fate and better able to influence events in the direction it wishes.

The impact of planning has been obvious on American policy since 1945. Although extemporizing in crisis situations is still a familiar aspect of American action, a steadily increasing number of moves bear the signs of being part of a reasonably well-articulated plan. The regrettable tendency to draw the planners into short-term projects has undoubtedly impaired their usefulness, but the centrality of their true role has been well recognized. The future will see increasing use made of specialists in long-range planning.

THE EXECUTIVE ESTABLISHMENT

Foreign policy may be conveniently broken down into four subcategories: political, military, economic, and psychological. In discussing the Department of State, we have been considering the purely political sector of the policy apparatus of the United States. In this section we shall look at the executive structures that operate within the remaining three areas. These will be, in order, the military, the economic, and the psychological arms of American policy. A final note on certain special-purpose agencies will follow.

THE MILITARY ARM   The American military establishment—the Department of Defense and the service departments of the Army, the Navy, and the Air Force—participates in general foreign-policy making and execution in addition to its special responsibility for the military security of the United States. The Department of Defense administers the military aid program to friendly states; an Assistant Secretary of Defense for International Security Affairs (ISA) has been charged with this function and with the development of the Department's position on broader questions of policy. He is assisted by a combined military and civilian staff; the former is drawn from all three services. Each of the uniformed services is organized for the political as well as the military aspects of the cold war.

From the National Security Council at the top to the least important interagency committee at the bottom, the Department of Defense is a key element in foreign-policy decisions. As its personnel have gained in knowledge and experience, they increasingly function as experts on general policy rather than simply as spokesmen for a military point of view. As such, their influence has steadily grown.

Military considerations affect American policy in another way. It is impossible today to disentangle matters of defense policy from international questions of broader import. The security of the United States demands overseas bases, forward deployment of American forces, elaborate alliance structures, military aid programs, and friendly and reliable governments abroad. Each of these and many other factors contribute to the overall foreign-policy problem of the nation, often in a highly immediate fashion. The development of an American policy on arms control, for example, has been very difficult because of the necessity to reconcile its security aspects with its more narrow diplomatic implications.

THE ECONOMIC ARM Diffusion rather than concentration marks the organization for economic foreign policy. Despite many proposals to unify these activities within a single agency, they remain widely scattered. Foreign economic and development assistance is the responsibility of the Agency for International Development, an autonomous unit of the Department of State. The Departments of Commerce, Agriculture, and Treasury each undertake particular missions under authorizing legislation. In addition, through American membership in the United Nations and a number of other international organizations, many objectives of American economic policy are served multilaterally.

In reality, this pluralism only reflects the nature of the case. The complexity of economic life offers literally uncounted opportunities for meaningful international action, and the organization for this effort must be as multiformed as the problem itself. The chief handicap of the present arrangement is the great administrative load it places on the President, and efforts to rationalize his foreign-policy responsibilities have all included some form of centralization of the foreign economic activities of the government. However it may be structured, it will always incorporate a bewildering variety of highly technical and very costly programs.

THE PROPAGANDA ARM Propaganda in the United States was once conceived as psychological warfare: a distinct sphere of public action aimed at winning victories by the exclusive use of psychological tools. Today, however, its function is more broadly conceived as the improvement of the world image of the nation, primarily in cultural and intellectual terms. Its direct role in policy support has been somewhat minimized but still remains important.

Although every foreign-policy official is in one sense a propagandist, direct responsibility for international propaganda belongs to the United States Information Agency (USIA). This independent agency, operating under the policy direction of the Department of State, develops and executes a great variety of informational programs abroad. Radio broadcasting (via the Voice of America), television programming, the distribution of press releases and "hard news," the supply of educational and artistic exhibits, the operation of American libraries and cultural centers abroad, the translation of American books into local languages, and widespread teaching of English are only some of the many tasks USIA carries on.

American opinions of USIA are mixed, and criticism balances praise. Undoubtedly many of its efforts have been ill-conceived, and much of its unfavorable publicity has been justified. But propaganda is not a cure-all, and part of the blame for poor American public relations abroad must rest upon poor policies conceived and executed by other agencies. The nature of USIA's mission is such that quick and measurable return on investment is very unlikely. The only true test of the Agency's worth will be the state of world opinion about American life and culture a generation hence.

SPECIAL-PURPOSE AGENCIES A few special agencies not within any Cabinet department nor directly involved in the conduct of relations with foreign states are nevertheless of great importance to the overall foreign-policy process in the United States. The first of these is the Atomic Energy Commission, whose broad range of activities includes the development of nuclear power for weapons and a stake in any form of nuclear arms control. A second is the National Aeronautics and Space Administration; the "space race" with the U.S.S.R. since 1957 has made NASA a vitally important participant in the cold-war effort of the United States. In a different category is the Central Intelligence Agency, whose mission is to coordinate and disseminate intelligence information and to conduct such intelligence activities of its own as can best be performed centrally. At times CIA has been well-publicized (as during the U-2 episode in 1960 and the Cuban invasion of 1961), but usually it operates under a cloak of deep secrecy.

CONGRESS AND FOREIGN POLICY

The new importance of foreign affairs to the formulation of public policy has had its effect on Congress. Both houses now devote a much larger share of their total time to international questions than formerly, since most of the policy moves of the United States call for congressional action at some point. The legislature's status relative to the President has improved as well, and for substantially the same reason: there is little done by the President in foreign policy that does not involve an appeal to Congress for support, legislation, or the appropriation of funds. If either house (or a committee of either house) finds itself at odds with the executive over a foreign-policy issue, the legislators can always gain a hearing for their position and on occasion can have their way at the President's expense.

But we should always keep in mind that Congress's new place in no way modifies the essential nature of its function. The power of *initiating* foreign policy remains an executive monopoly, and even the most interested and active Congress can do no more than *react* to Presidential leadership. Congress may reject an executive project, it may modify it in detail or even in fundamentals, it may volubly express its dismay. It cannot, however, force the President to adopt a policy with which he is not in sympathy. Congress has indeed become an integral part of the foreign-policy process, and in importance it is now virtually the equal of the executive. Its function, however, is specialized and complements the President's power rather than superseding it.

TREATIES AND APPOINTMENTS   The two most immediate foreign-affairs powers of Congress are constitutionally reserved to the Senate: the approval of treaties and the confirmation of appointments.

A treaty (negotiated, we recall, by executive authority) must be submitted to the Senate for approval before the President is allowed to ratify (sign) it and declare it in effect. Senate approval must be by a two-thirds vote of those present and voting. The "treaty veto" of the Senate, much publicized at the close of World War I, is a constant danger although seldom exercised in recent years. The role of the Senate is limited to acceptance or rejection; if it proposes amendments, these are without effect unless the President chooses to renegotiate the treaty in terms satisfactory to the Senate. Nor, for that matter, is the President bound to ratify a treaty even after Senate approval. He may change his mind (or circumstances themselves may have made the treaty inappropriate) and decide to let the entire project lapse.

Much less controversial is the Senate's role in foreign-policy appointments. Only a majority vote is required, and—although many executive appointments in other fields are contested—the Senate allows the President a relatively free hand in selecting his foreign-policy advisers and assistants. Occasionally a political payoff in the form of an ambassadorship is seriously questioned. The usual outcome of such a dispute is the withdrawal of the nomination by the President and the substitution of someone more acceptable.

LEGISLATION Congress's basic function—legislation—bears directly on foreign policy in several ways. In the first place, the elaboration and reorganization of the governmental machinery for foreign affairs is a legislative prerogative; every executive officer except the President and Vice President owes his position to an act of Congress. Second, Congress passes many authorization acts: measures that state an objective, stake out guidelines to action, and authorize the President or his subordinates to move toward the goal. These enactments give rise to "programs": continuing efforts toward long-range goals that require implementation over a period of years. The third form of legislation is the one-time operation that accomplishes a single immediate purpose. By far, the larger number of legislative acts affecting foreign policy are of this type.

In legislating, Congress has a real advantage over the executive, for he—except for his veto threat—must accept what comes to him. By means of the publicity which surrounds floor debate and especially committee hearings, full public attention is focused on an issue and its different interpretations. Most executive requests for legislation, as a matter of fact, are to some significant extent modified by Congress, although only rarely are they rejected outright. The President, after all, has political and public-relations resources of his own, and few Congressmen care to be drawn into open defiance of the Chief Executive.

APPROPRIATIONS The key status of Congress is most obvious when it appropriates funds for foreign policy. No governmental expenditures may be made without an appropriation act, and the legislative branch has long cherished its whip hand over the supply of money. Congress, in the tradition of independent legislatures everywhere in the world, makes annual appropriations for most objects, thus ensuring itself an annual review of the multitude of government functions. It has not departed from this practice in financing national defense and foreign aid, in spite of many executive suggestions that it appropriate funds for some longer period in the interests of continuity of policy. Each year congressional review results in some change in the programs as the members capitalize on the opportunity to indulge their pet enthusiasms or prejudices.

Legislative control over funds also forces executive officials to go through the long drawn-out budget cycle, featured by hearings before the Appropriations Committees of both houses. Here embarrassing and annoying questions are certain to be asked; here also Congress discovers many things that the executive departments would much prefer be kept hidden. The interbranch tension intrinsic to any system of separation of powers is never more clearly demonstrated than during budget hearings. Out of the whole process will emerge an appropriation bill that has been cut down from the original request, sometimes intelligently but more often by means of what is inelegantly called the "meat-ax."

INVESTIGATIONS   The power to investigate in order to gain information preparatory to legislating is a congressional prerogative of great relevance to foreign policy. Of course, usually the recommendation of legislation is not the prime purpose of an investigation. Sometimes a committee investigates in order to uncover the facts of a confused situation; sometimes the object is to fix the blame for a failure of policy. Occasionally an investigation is admittedly a fishing expedition to see what embarrassing disclosures can be made. Some famous investigations were above all vehicles for the political aggrandizement of the committee or its chairman.

A committee inquiry receives wide publicity and news coverage. The rules of a free press being what they are, it is inevitable that the most sensational charges, conflicts, and findings will receive the greatest attention. The chief casualties of a congressional investigation into foreign policy are usually the public's sense of proportion and perspective and the ability of the responsible officials to perform their tasks confidently and efficiently. So potentially devastating have investigations become that occasionally the mere suggestion that one might be undertaken is enough to bring the menaced bureaucrats to terms with their congressional opponents.

PUBLICITY In the last analysis congressional influence over foreign policy is much greater than its specific powers might suggest. This is largely because Congress—especially the House of Representatives—is a supremely political body, alert to the electoral implications of everything it does. This makes Congress much more responsive to public (voter) opinion than is a career civil servant. One weapon of the democratic politician is publicity, and the members of Congress are supreme in their ability to make political capital out of well-timed manipulation of deeply felt foreign policy symbols.

A sampling of what members of Congress are saying about foreign affairs provides a fairly accurate estimate of public attitudes as of that moment. If a President cannot convince Congress of the desirability or the necessity of a proposed policy, it is probable that he does not have adequate support within the general public. It might be argued that this political trait of Congress, its constant testing of the political acceptability of programs and policies, is its most important contribution to the maintenance of an effective rapport between the people and their government.

OVERSEAS REPRESENTATION

American foreign policy is implemented by a variety of representatives who serve outside the boundaries of the United States. These emissaries are of several types, corresponding to the several channels of policy we noted earlier: diplomatic, military, economic, and informational.

THE AMERICAN MISSION There is, in each country with which the United States maintains relations, a chief American representative. He is, in all but a handful of instances, the Ambassador of the United States. As chief of mission, he is in charge of all American diplomatic and consular personnel stationed in the country, and is operationally responsible for the direction of the work of all other official representatives of the United States there. A decade or more ago, his primacy was not recognized, and heads of American military or economic missions virtually ignored him and operated independently. This issue, however, has been finally settled and the Ambassador, representing the entire nation on behalf of the Department of State, is clearly the senior American representative in the host country.

In the Embassy of the United States is located the Ambassador's staff. He is assisted by subordinate officers with various functional specializations in administrative, political, economic, and other important areas. Also forming part of his staff are the various attachés—military, naval, air, labor, agriculture, science, and others—who are not employees of the Department of State and who report back to their own departments. The overseas posts of the USIA (known abroad as the United States Information Service) are also under the supervision of the Ambassador. The country chief of the USIS is known as the Public Affairs Officer and also serves on the Ambassador's personal staff.

Ambassadorial duties have changed during the past generation, due especially to the improvements in transportation and communication. Negotiation is much less important than in earlier days, but accurate and speedy reporting is much more so. Whereas formerly Ambassadors were expected largely to confine their contacts to other diplomats and to officials of the host government, today public relations in the broadest and best sense is a major responsibility. Becoming widely known and respected by the people of the host nation is crucial to the success of most American chiefs of mission.

THE FOREIGN SERVICE   The diplomatic and consular personnel of an American mission are members of the Foreign Service of the United States, a distinct career service independent of the regular Civil Service. These men and women spend their careers in the representation of the United States abroad and (in recent years) in manning most of the policy-making posts in the Department of State. A member of the Foreign Service may look forward hopefully to crowning his career with an appointment as an Ambassador. Prior to that time he will have filled many important posts abroad and in the Department (the Assistant Secretaries in charge of geographic bureaus have in recent years generally been Foreign Service officers). The Foreign Service, with its traditions of dedication and efficiency, compares favorably to the diplomatic corps of any other nation. The United States is consistently well served by its diplomats abroad.

MILITARY REPRESENTATION   American military representation abroad is of several types. Service attachés are a familiar part of every American diplomatic mission; they deal with the military establishment of their host governments. In nations with which the United States has a military assistance agreement in force, a Military Assistance Advisory Group (MAAG) composed of uniformed personnel works with the host government in preparing and administering requests to Washington for shipments of matériel. In several states the United States has training missions to instruct the local forces in the effective employment of the military equipment transferred from the United States under the aid program. Finally, we must mention American military installations overseas as being special forms of representation, particularly the headquarters staff working within such multinational commands as the North Atlantic Treaty Organization.

ECONOMIC REPRESENTATION Although all the many agencies of the American government that have an international economic function make use of overseas representatives, the most numerous are the missions of the Agency for International Development. AID administers nonmilitary (economic) aid to friendly nations, and AID economic specialists are to be found in several dozen foreign states. The AID mission, although quite self-contained and directly under the control of the Director of AID in Washington, is still under the day-by-day direction of the resident American Ambassador. The same is true of any additional commercial, financial, or other economic representatives who may be permanently stationed in the particular country.

INFORMATIONAL AND CULTURAL REPRESENTATION Next to the diplomatic corps, USIA has the most elaborate and widespread network of overseas missions. In each state where USIA operates, a Public Affairs Officer is in charge. He usually has two principal subordinates, a Cultural Affairs Officer charged with dealing with the intellectual community, and a Press Officer who maintains good relations with the local press. He may also have an Educational Exchange Officer to administer the various programs of educational exchange.

Below this central headquarters is a more or less elaborate network of subposts: information centers, libraries, news bureaus, "binational centers," and the like. An American employee of USIA is almost always in charge of each of these, assisted often by a small American staff but always relying heavily on local personnel. Each subpost operates under the control of the country PAO in standard administrative fashion. The USIA's responsibility, in contrast to that of the other forms of representation, lies almost entirely in direct contacts with the public of the host nation, and its personnel must therefore develop great skill in cross-cultural communication if their efforts are to have any success.

Review Questions

1. What are the sources of the President's power in foreign policy?

2. What is the nature of the relationship between the President and his Secretary of State?

3. Compare the foreign-policy roles of the Department of State and the Department of Defense.

4. What are the ways in which Congress influences foreign policy?

5. What is the Foreign Service of the United States?

6. What are the different types of overseas representation of the United States?

THE COLD WAR

Chapter 5

Since the end of World War II, the major problem of American foreign policy—as all Americans know—has been the conduct of the cold war with the Soviet Union and the Communist bloc. The threat from Moscow has been so fearsome and manysided that it has served as the point of departure for virtually everything that the United States has thought and done in world affairs. Many other problems of great complexity and difficulty have faced the nation since 1945, but none has rivaled the cold war in duration, in intensity, or in danger. The story of American foreign policy in the contemporary era, in other words, is primarily the history of the struggle against Communist expansion.

THE NATURE OF THE THREAT

The task of the United States has been complicated by the fact that the challenge from the Soviet is without parallel in American experience. In versatility, in persistence, in ubiquity, and in capacity for harm the U.S.S.R. surpasses any previous adversary of the United States. Americans, in spite of their acquisition of a considerable fund of experience with the problem of the Soviet, has been unable fully to clear the first obstacle to effective foreign policy: a mastery of the true dimensions of the task they face and of the real requirements it imposes. The threat from Moscow is simultaneously complex and direct, and neither incantations nor hasty violence are sufficient to turn it back. After a decade and a half, Americans still swing between overestimation and underestimation of Soviet power and Soviet intentions. American policy, therefore, often attempts far more than is necessary or possible in one situation while taking only weak and futile action in another. A realistic assessment of the danger must be the first American step in the development of a successful policy.

COMMUNIST IDEOLOGY   For most Americans the problem of American foreign policy is simple: the United States is to "stop Communism." The overwhelming feature of the cold war has been that it is a conflict with an ideology that denies the very foundations of a free society and predicts its own inevitable victory throughout the world. The danger from Russia is great enough in itself; formulated as it usually is in the terms and concepts of Communist doctrine, it seems to become an engine of monstrous menace.

There is no need here to repeat the elements of Communist thought. Elaborate and scholarly analyses are conveniently available for anyone who is interested in the contemporary manifestations of the ideology. Directly germane to our purpose, however, are two questions that bear upon it: First, to what extent does Communism actually govern the actions of the Kremlin hierarchy? Second, what is the relationship between revolutionary doctrine and the realities of power politics in Soviet foreign policy?

The Kremlin, of course, insists that everything it does flows from a central ideological source. Were we to take these arguments at face value—as many Americans do—the first question would answer itself. Soviet policy would be no more than a blind application of inflexible ideological imperatives. The Communist line has undergone too many reversals and alterations, however, and too many instances can be cited of Soviet action directly contradictory to Marxist thought, for us to accept any such simple thesis.

The history of Soviet behavior indicates strongly that Communist thought undoubtedly affects the way Moscow interprets particular problems, but that in the final analysis the U.S.S.R. bases its action on highly realistic calculations of power and interest. The role of ideology in shaping Soviet purposes is less clear. No one is absolutely certain whether "world Communism" is a clear goal of Soviet policy or merely a cloak for more opportunistic and indeterminate objectives. Americans, in a word, cannot ignore ideology in attempting to evaluate the U.S.S.R., but neither are they justified in myopically concentrating upon it.

Much more important, in any case, is the use of ideology as a tool of Soviet foreign policy. The Kremlin has been very successful in identifying Communism with revolutionary change in many parts of the world. Here Communism has come to stand for the elimination of political, social, and economic exploitation and the Soviet Union poses as the friend of the underprivileged everywhere. This has been one of Moscow's most successful maneuvers, and the United States has had great difficulty in devising an effective response to it.

THE SOVIET BLOC Moscow is today the capital of an enormous empire, and the leader of a massive power bloc in world politics. In addition to the vast expanse of the U.S.S.R. itself, the Soviet camp includes in Europe, Poland, East Germany, Czechoslovakia, Hungary, Bulgaria, Romania, and Albania; in Asia, Communist China, North Korea, and Vietminh (north Vietnam). All these states have Communist government and only China and Albania conduct independent foreign policies. As of early 1963, a number of other states in other parts of the world have shown leanings toward the Soviet bloc; Cuba under Fidel Castro has gone so far as openly to identify itself as a Soviet satellite. In addition, the U.S.S.R. steadily probes weaknesses in the non-Communist world, seeking to topple neutral or pro-Western regimes and to replace them with Communist governments that would join the Soviet bloc.

The Soviet camp is thus both large and powerful, and provides a solid base for an active world role. The Kremlin has not been slow to capitalize upon it.

SOVIET OBJECTIVES AND TECHNIQUES Soviet objectives in the cold-war era fall into three broad categories. First, the U.S.S.R. is grimly determined to guarantee its own security and the stability of its regime against all threats from the outside world. Second, the Kremlin is insistent upon gaining full recognition as a great power from all other states, with all that that implies with regard to totality of interests, military power, regional hegemony, and maximized prestige. Third, Moscow is eager to expand its sphere of influence and seeks to do so at any place and time a favorable opportunity presents itself.

It has been the third category of action that has brought the Soviet into collision most forcibly with the United States. America is not a natural security threat to the Soviet Union, nor does the United States really object to accepting the U.S.S.R. as a great power. But in its program of expansion, inaugurated in the aftermath of World War II and followed ever since, the Soviet Union has created the conditions that have led to the cold war. American policy, as we shall see in a moment, is aimed at arresting Soviet ambitions without necessarily depriving it either of security or of global status.

Soviet foreign-policy techniques are a curious amalgam of the old and the new. The U.S.S.R. carries on diplomacy and foreign relations in the classic tradition, but combines the familiar apparatus with several elements of its own devising. Among the more striking Soviet techniques we may note the following: (1) an incessant drumfire of propaganda in all media; (2) the subversion of unfriendly or neutral government by local Communist parties; (3) a blatant use of military threats, known in the West as "missile rattling"; (4) the mobilization of proxy forces in civil or guerrilla wars to serve Soviet ends; (5) a naked reliance on economic pressure, either coercively or as a bribe; (6) an open prestige competition with the West and particularly with the United States for the adherence of the uncommitted peoples. These, coupled with the support of the satellite nations, give Moscow a tremendously versatile battery of techniques.

SOVIET IMPERIALISM   The expansion of Soviet influence into a state has in fact two immediate consequences: the attempted imposition of Communist social, economic, and political systems, and a complete subservience to Russian foreign policy. The U.S.S.R. cannot content itself with allies, but must have satellites. Any small state caught in the Soviet orbit stands in great danger of being forced to make itself into a miniature replica of the U.S.S.R. itself and to become a mere instrument of Kremlin world policy. Although the forms of independence are preserved and much verbal deference is paid to nationalism, Soviet-bloc states are victims of as vicious a form of imperialism as that prevalent during the height of European colonialism.

All true satellites, however, today lie on the periphery of the U.S.S.R. or the bloc. Noncontiguous states suffering Communist pressure have one advantage: they are not subject to the immediate threat of the Red Army. They can therefore—if they wish to—mount an effective defense against "satellitization." Several smaller states—Burma, the United Arab Republic, and Ghana are examples—have done so in recent years. Their success in holding back the Kremlin argues that Soviet imperialism can be fully successful only when it realizes its military component. No purely political-psychological-economic thrust can succeed fully in the face of determined opposition. Lately the United States has realized this inhibition on Soviet imperialism and has moved to strengthen resistance efforts in several threatened states.

The nonideological orientation of Soviet imperialism is clearly demonstrated by the cases of Yugoslavia and Finland. The former, admittedly Communist, is sometimes an opponent and never a close ally of the Soviet, while Finland, although completely under Moscow's thumb in foreign policy, is nevertheless permitted to retain its free society and democratic government. The crucial test of acceptability in Soviet eyes is not the official ideology of a state but rather its orientation toward the international position of the U.S.S.R. Small states are "satellitized," therefore, more in order to guarantee foreign-policy support for the Kremlin than in response to any uncomplicated urge to spread Communist gospel.

THE PROBLEM OF RED CHINA   Probably the most troublesome aspect of the entire Communist threat is the future of China. Under Communist rule since 1949 (except for Taiwan) and with soaring ambitions and rising power, China obviously is evolving toward a new status. Its place within the Soviet bloc has become unclear and it demands consideration in its own right.

The Peiping regime is making a massive effort to mobilize all China's resources for a breakout into major status in the world—something China has never enjoyed. Technological and economic advances marred by failure and famine, military strength, and an adventurous leadership made China a significant force in world affairs within a decade after the victory of Communism. There is a dynamism and recklessness in Chinese policy that—considering the tense state of international relations today—cannot help but be disquieting.

Communist China makes the entire non-Western world its hunting ground. Attempting to epitomize the "revolution of rising expectations" in the minds of Asians, Africans, and Latin Americans, it has won adherents and spread its influence widely. Particularly remarkable has been the speed and versatility with which Mao Tse-tung and his associates have capitalized on situations of internal instability and international weakness in many parts of the world.

The United States is, of course, deeply perplexed about the impact of Chinese adventurism on world stability; many experts claim that Peiping is an even more serious peril than is Moscow. But it has lately become clear that the Soviet itself is disturbed about the rise of China. The leader–satellite relationship has been dissolved in open rivalry as Mao aspires to leadership of the Communist world. This trend within the Communist bloc obviously will affect its overall approach to the rest of the world and will in turn present American policy makers with a radically changed situation.

AMERICAN GOALS AND OBJECTIVES

The American response to the Soviet threat has been portrayed to the public as a series of unrelated crisis operations to beat back individual thrusts by the Kremlin. There is some truth in this picture, for American policy is by no means as integrated and consistent as it might be and perhaps should be. The impression that the United States expends most of its effort in reacting negatively to Soviet initiatives, however, should not obscure the fact that the United States has its own goals and objectives as well. A review of these purposes will give some greater perspective to our later discussion.

THE NEUTRALIZATION OF THE THREAT   Of highest priority in American thinking is the neutralization of the Soviet threat. Moscow's aggressive behavior must be curbed and the Kremlin brought to the realization of the futility of its course of action before the United States can proceed to the accomplishment of any of its other purposes. This effort has occupied the greatest share of American energy since 1946.

The policy to achieve this objective has been known for many years as containment. On the basis of the old psychological principle that to change a person's behavior one must first frustrate him, the United States has set itself to obstruct every Soviet attempt at expansion. In whatever part of the world the U.S.S.R. may seek to increase its empire or by whatever means it may choose to act, there the United States is bound to appear in opposition. The implementation of this policy has led America to conclude military alliances in Europe, to support United Nations action in Africa, to engage in proxy guerrilla activities in Southeast Asia, and to undertake large-scale and long-term development aid projects in Latin America. In each case, in spite of unique conditions that impose great variety on the techniques the United States adopts, the motivation of frustrating Soviet, expansion has been a constant element.

THE STABILIZATION OF RELATIONSHIPS   The dramatic quality and frequent urgency of the pursuit of the first American objective has tended to downgrade the other cold-war aims of the United States. Merely to say "no" to the U.S.S.R. is not enough, however satisfying it may be to bruised American egos. If Soviet behavior is ever to be changed, the United States must be prepared with a set of objectives appropriate to the new situation.

This is why the formula of "stop Communism" is inadequate, for what is the United States to do after Communism is stopped? It is in no sense utopian to prepare a plan of action for such a situation, for it may arise at any moment. Some idea of eventual purpose, furthermore, must govern day-by-day operational decisions in active theaters of the cold war. If, for example, the ultimate goal of the United States is the destruction of the Soviet Union and the total extirpation of Communism, American tacticians will follow a different line than if some more limited victory is being sought.

Based both on statements made by American leaders since 1946 and on the logic of American action, it is clear that the next phase of United States policy after the neutralization of the Soviet threat calls for the stabilization of Soviet-American relationships on some basis of mutual toleration. Americans demand neither that the U.S.S.R. vanish nor that it be converted to democracy and capitalism (although either outcome would not be really unwelcome), but rather only that Moscow give convincing proof that it intends to live in a tolerable state of peaceful coexistence with the United States.

This may be put in terms of an American attempt to bring the U.S.S.R. to accept a set of limits on its action, particularly in its relations with the United States, that are analogous to those the United States itself accepts. These ground rules will have the effect of keeping disagreements and conflicts well below the level of explosion and thus improve the likelihood of everyone's survival. Conflict—possibly of long duration—between Moscow and the free world is most probable under any circumstances; the best that anyone can hope for is a system whereby the controversies can be safely managed and brought to mutually acceptable conclusions. The United States is deeply committed to this type of stabilized relationship with the U.S.S.R. and assumes both its possibility and its desirability.

THE REDUCTION OF TENSIONS Both the U.S.S.R. and the United States often protest their interest in a reduction of tensions between the two countries, and each professes to blame the other for the fact that the cold war remains tense. Although the stabilization of relationships we have just discussed undoubtedly would entail a lowering of the overall tension level, it is unrealistic to pursue a reduction of tensions as an end in itself.

Tension between two great states is not itself a cause of difficulty, but rather a symptom of it. The unproductive and dangerous state of Soviet-American relations grows out of disagreement over specific problems and from these disagreements, prosecuted in the field of action, grows the tension that bemuses the world. A *détente* cannot be achieved by any mutual act of will in which both sides will say—and mean— "Let us henceforth be less tense!" It can come about only by the piecemeal dismantling of the edifice of conflict that stands between the two states today.

To bring any such eventuality about, however, would require good will on both sides and at least a modicum of good faith to provide the bases of the initial agreements that would reverse the spiral of crisis. Only if Americans can be absolutely certain that the United States has in its own conduct clearly demonstrated its own good will and good faith can they be justified in blaming the cold war entirely on the U.S.S.R. The Kremlin has been aggressive, hostile, and suspicious; can the United States be sure that such behavior has been without any justification in American policy? Much of the world, Americans have recently learned to their dismay, distributes the blame rather impartially to both cold-war camps.

The United States, moreover, must guard against one danger. Americans distrust everything the U.S.S.R. says. Just because Moscow advocates peaceful coexistence and the reduction of tensions, there is a temptation for the United States to reject both ideas as only propaganda cloaks for sinister Communist designs. This is literally an impossible position. What other bearable alternatives to the cold war can be suggested? Coexistence and lowered tensions would seem to be no more than tritely verbalized minima for a satisfactory escape from the cold war. The fact that the Soviet urges them makes the ideas no less intrinsically worthy. It behooves the United States to work realistically for their realization on acceptable terms rather than to reject them root and branch with no clear idea of what to put in their place as goals.

THE LONG-RANGE GOAL: PEACE   Put into almost utopian language, the long-range purpose for which the United States strives may be expressed in one word: peace. By this word is meant more than the mere absence of war but rather a more broadly conceived set of relationships. It does not go so far, however, as to imply the total triumph of reason and the disappearance of conflict and disagreement among nations. Peace as an American objective has two meanings, one procedural and the other substantive.

Procedurally, a peaceful world is one in which the change that is so necessary to orderly political life takes place without recourse to war. This requires first that legal, moral, political, and practical inhibitions be placed upon the use of war as a tool of policy. But merely to make war impossible (or overwhelmingly inexpedient) is not enough. There must also be, in a peaceful world, a set of efficacious and accepted alternatives to war by means of which states may gain the satisfactions and the escape from frustration that war formerly supplied.

Substantively, peace will mean a world in which the needs, wants, and urges of men are sufficiently satisfied that the vast bulk of them will be more interested in preserving the distribution of rewards than they will be in upsetting it. Conflicts will occur even in such an arrangement, of course, but the common stake in preserving the system would ensure that they would find their eventual resolution within safe limits.

It seems scarcely necessary to point out that the actualization of this concept of peace lies far in the future, if indeed it has any reality at all. But it serves as a very useful target at which the United States may aim and as a yardstick to govern the choice among action alternatives. Thus, the well-established transforming instinct of American foreign policy once again finds expression: the United States is still seeking some more rational and logical base for relations than the traditional one of power politics. Woodrow Wilson, in other words, still has a message for Americans.

AMERICAN COLD-WAR TECHNIQUES

In the prosecution of the cold war the United States takes advantage of every available technique. The long-term effort against the Soviet threat has assumed so many forms that America has had to develop a large battery of devices, many of them unprecedented to international politics and all of them of a magnitude and duration unsuspected when the cold war began. In spite of the complexity of the American action program, however, it is clear that even more imaginative and extensive techniques are required to meet the demands of the future.

MILITARY DEFENSE   The most expensive and the most critical of American foreign-policy techniques is military defense. The United States has assumed the continuing obligation of maintaining a huge military establishment in a state of constant readiness. Approximately 50 billion dollars is spent annually on defense, and there is constant anxiety that even this enormous expenditure is inadequate.

The military problem of the United States is twofold. In the first place, the nation must retain the ability to cope with direct Communist aggression against the United States by seeking to deter any attack or, if deterrence fails, by defeating such enemy forces as come against it. Second, the United States needs military power to reinforce its foreign policy in dealing with the Soviet bloc, the neutrals, or even its own allies. This dual responsibility has raised many problems of doctrine, strategy, deployment, and allocation of resources.

Basically the United States rests its deterrent case on an extensive armory of nuclear weapons with a variety of delivery systems—aircraft, missiles, artillery, and the like. These are "strategic" weapons whose operational purpose is the total annihilation of the enemy. Below this umbrella of total war capability the nation maintains forces of lesser destructive potential, designed to apply force in variable amounts according to doctrines of "graduated deterrence," "flexible response," or "limited war." The precise relationships between the two types of military power is a matter of hot controversy; defense policy is constantly debated in the United States.

SECURITY PACTS   The security threat posed by the Soviet bloc can be met effectively only by joint action. To permit Moscow to pick off the free world one state at a time would be the acme of fatuity. The United States has therefore taken the lead in developing collective defense arrangements throughout the free world and today is the center of a web of security pacts that put America in alliance with 43 states, divided as follows:

1. *North Atlantic Treaty Organization (NATO)*. United States, Canada, United Kingdom, France, West Germany, Italy, Norway, Denmark, Iceland, Belgium, the Netherlands, Luxembourg, Portugal, Greece, and Turkey.

2. *Organization of American States (OAS)*. United States and the 20 Latin American republics (less Cuba).

3. *Southeast Asia Treaty Organization (SEATO)*. United States, United Kingdom, France, Australia, New Zealand, Pakistan, Thailand, and the Philippines.

4. *Australia–New Zealand–United States (ANZUS)*.

5. *Central Treaty Organization (CENTO)*. United Kingdom, Turkey, Iran, and Pakistan; the United States "cooperates" but is not formally a member.

6. *Bilateral pacts*. The United States has bilateral treaties with Japan, the Republic of Korea, Nationalist China on Taiwan, and the Philippines, and has a special agreement with Spain. Aid is also extended to Yugoslavia on the basis of informal understandings.

Although the details differ, all the pacts provide for United States intervention into a military crisis involving any of its allies and for cooperation in meeting the threat. The United States has found these agreements indispensable in developing responses to Soviet expansion.

FOREIGN MILITARY ASSISTANCE   As part of its attempt to strengthen the defenses of the free world, the United States has extended military assistance to its allies and to various noncommitted states in whose military capacity America has an interest. Assistance takes either of two forms: direct aid, in the form of military end-items (the "hardware" itself), and "defense support," defined as economic assistance which enables the recipient state better to maintain its own defenses.

Military assistance has been or is being given to more than 50 countries. During the decade 1950–1960, 25.4 billion dollars was expended in this way, over half going to the NATO allies in Europe. France received the largest total amount of aid of all (4.4 billion dollars), followed by Taiwan, Italy, Turkey, and South Korea in that order.

A characteristic of the military aid program has been the close relationship between the amount of American aid and the immediacy of the Soviet threat. A sudden increase in Soviet pressure in an area automatically results in a major step-up in American military assistance. The Middle East, for example, became the major recipient of military aid after the Soviet appeared in the region after 1955; the Castro crisis in Cuba produced similar reactions in Washington after 1959 as the United States moved to strengthen its Latin American allies.

ECONOMIC AND DEVELOPMENT ASSISTANCE   Economic assistance to friendly countries is a major nonmilitary channel for American cold-war policy. It draws its inspiration from the obvious fact that economic discontent and stagnation in a country provides fertile ground for Communist propaganda and that on the contrary a healthy economy is an effective barrier against Soviet penetration.

The first great American effort in this field was the Marshall Plan, initiated in 1948 to aid the states of Western Europe rebuild their shattered industrial plants. For four years the United States poured a total of over 17 billion dollars into Europe; by 1952 the task was completed and European recovery assured. The focus of attention then shifted to the non-Western world.

Here the problem was different. Instead of rehabilitating preexisting industrial systems, it was necessary to develop new ones. The non-Western world has been gripped by the famous "revolution of rising expectations" and as early as 1949 (in the Point Four proposal in President Truman's inaugural address) the United States realized that long-range programs for economic development would offer the nation a unique opportunity. The U.S.S.R. sensed the rewards to be gained by assisting in the development of backward economies, and development aid acquired a cold-war dimension. Today there is open competition between Moscow and Washington in the game of aiding and financing development programs.

The supply of finished goods (except for military and defense-support items) has dwindled to a trickle in the total flow of American aid. The chief concern now is with two problems growing out of the worldwide urge for development. The first is the necessity to supply the technical knowledge necessary to work such a peaceful revolution in primitive economies, and the second is the provision of the large amounts of capital needed to make development a reality. The United States attacks the first by a number of technical assistance programs, of which the recent Peace Corps is a well-publicized example. The second is approached via a certain amount of direct grants voted by Congress, by means of American financing agencies such as the Export-Import

Bank and the AID, and by American membership in international bodies charged with the same mission: the World Bank, the International Finance Corporation, the International Development Agency, and the European-American Organization for Economic Cooperation and Development (OECD).

In addition, we should note other special programs of economic aid, including "Food for Peace"—the international distribution of surplus agricultural stocks held by the United States government—and the regular American membership in the United Nations and other international organizations with an economic orientation.

The total cost of economic assistance between 1945 and 1962 came to approximately 85 billion dollars. For this not inconsiderable amount the United States received real dividends in the form of stabilized allies and neutrals better able to resist Communist pressure. Economic aid of all sorts is obviously destined to play a part in American foreign policy for many years.

DIPLOMATIC AND PROPAGANDA WARFARE   The techniques discussed up to this point are all aimed at strengthening the non-Communist world in its dealings with the Soviet bloc. The focus of direct Soviet-American relations is much less complex.

The United States proceeds on the assumption of a lack of community of interest with the U.S.S.R., and every contact is actually or potentially a hostile one. Thus "diplomatic warfare" is a not inapt term to apply to routine political encounters with the Soviet, as American negotiators attempt to wrest a measurable victory from each struggle. The United States learned this lesson from the Soviets themselves in the early postwar period. Today reaching an agreement on the basis of a satisfactory compromise (traditionally a major function of diplomacy) is subordinated in practice to the aim of strengthening an American position or weakening a Soviet one.

Diplomacy therefore becomes a technique of struggle rather than a method of escaping from it. Its major utility is for propaganda; negotiation is used to embarrass the Soviet before the world audience, while the U.S.S.R. attempts to do the same thing to the United States. Even meetings at the "summit" involving heads of government, in spite of the fanfares of publicity that surround them, are not used to resolve differences but as lofty propaganda platforms.

Propaganda war is a major technique of American policy, although not a spectacularly successful one. The United States seeks to propagandize (although in different ways) the Communist world, the neutrals, the other states of the Western bloc, and the American people. The Soviet, of course, aims at the same targets in reverse with its propaganda. For the United States the propaganda campaign is carried on mainly by the United States Information Agency. The struggle goes on incessantly, but overall it is generally considered a draw. Many analysts, however, give the Soviet Union a slight edge because of its more ambitious program and greater diligence.

ECONOMIC WARFARE   The United States has largely abandoned economic warfare as a technique of the Soviet-American conflict. Early in the cold war there were hopes that boycotts, interruption of trade, and other coercive economic moves might cause serious tensions within the Soviet bloc. The rapid economic growth of the U.S.S.R. has shattered these dreams. Although East-West trade remains at a low level, this situation has very little effect on the course of the cold war. The Soviet in recent years has repeatedly suggested an increase in trade, but without eliciting any encouraging response from the United States. Other members of the Western alliance, however, have shown keen interest in building up the volume of trade across the Iron Curtain.

STATUS AND PRESTIGE COMPETITION   Ever since the Soviet Union launched the first space satellite in 1957, the cold war has become a struggle for prestige. This evidence that the U.S.S.R. had led the way in an area in which the United States had assumed its automatic primacy suddenly made Americans very anxious about the image they were projecting to the world. In recent years the prestige race has been perhaps the most important feature of the cold war to the United States.

It is difficult to be precise about the matter of prestige. If the United States demands a perpetually subordinate world status for the U.S.S.R. as a price of peace, then the prestige struggle is as good as lost. The Soviet has already claimed and made good its right to major status. But it is not so clear that the high prestige of the U.S.S.R. in any material way reduces that of the United States—except perhaps in American eyes. Is it true that nothing less than absolute and unique supremacy is either America's natural due or the only way to guarantee the security of the United States?

Certain troublesome questions also arise regarding the components of prestige. Just what is it in which the Soviet and the United States are rivals? It is widely believed that the U.S.S.R. has a lead in the space race and the United States is striving to catch up. America, however, has a huge lead in individual standards of living—and the Soviet in turn is hoping to catch up. Which accomplishment produces the greater increment of prestige? Of the same sort is the issue of the audience: In whose eyes does the United States hope to appear prestigious? There are indications that the world thinks no less of America because it is not first in space or in economic growth rate, but that the major disillusionment has taken place among Americans themselves. The prestige issue is at bottom a search for external reassurances to quiet domestic anxiety and dismay. If this is true, it is difficult to escape the conclusion that the whole matter is a dangerous and frivolous digression from the really important business of the nation.

TRENDS IN THE COLD WAR

The cold war has not been a single entity, an unbroken era of constant struggle. There have been distinct phases within it, marked by the ascendancy of various trends. In this section we shall examine these major trends without attempting a strict chronological summary of the course of events.

THE TWO-CAMP PRINCIPLE   As the Soviet-American struggle became stabilized after 1946, the organizing principle upon which the United States based its policy was known as bipolarity—the doctrine of the two camps. This concept held that there were only two power centers in the world, Moscow and Washington, and only one important issue: the relations between them. Every state and people must join one side or the other and relate their own concerns to the overriding demands of the cold war. No problem was worth serious consideration except in so far as it fitted into the cold-war context.

This simple formulation of world affairs dominated American action between 1946 and the early phases of the Korean War. During this era the United States sought to eliminate "power vacuums" (uncommitted states) and to draw a clear line between the two camps. Washington worked steadily to unify the non-Communist world into a single anti-Soviet military and political bloc. This was the rationale for the military and economic aid programs initiated at this time. The concept of the "free world" gained currency as a symbol of opposition to Moscow.

Like so much American cold-war thinking, this whole idea was no more than an inversion of the standard Communist dogma of the division of the world into socialist and imperialist camps. It was most valuable in providing a framework within which the United States could move to build collective defense within the non-Communist world, but it suffered from one serious inhibition: it suggested no action program against the Soviet other than the unpalatable alternatives of preventive war or intolerable but perpetual stalemate. Containment was at the height of its popularity at this time, but as it became an end in itself it ossified and gave American policy a rigidity it has never lost.

The premises of the two-camp principle were washed away by the rise of neutralism after 1952. American policy no longer assumes that the cold war is its only international business or that all the members of the free world share equally in the wish for an American-type "victory" over the Soviet. But although policy is no longer made in these terms, the semantics of bipolarity live on. Public and political discussion still use 1947-type ideas; no changes are alleged to have occurred in the Kremlin since the death of Stalin. The United States is still struggling with the bipolar concept.

THE RISE OF NEUTRALISM   Since the initial breakaway of Yugoslavia in 1948 and India in 1951, many states have taken the path of neutralism: a secession from the bipolar world and participation in the cold war. Today perhaps a majority of states do not accept membership in either camp but develop their policy exclusively in terms of their own interests. Neutralism has become an accepted aspect of world politics.

The neutrals exist because the mutually frustrating nature of Soviet-American relations gives small states an unsuspected freedom of action. Neither Moscow nor Washington—at least since the U.S.S.R. acted in Hungary in 1956—is willing to take the risk involved in subduing a neutral. Their ranks have been swollen by the appearance of many new states in Asia and Africa, almost all of which are determined to avoid being sucked into the maelstrom of great-power conflict. The loosening of intrabloc ties on both sides of the Iron Curtain has also given rise to additional potential converts to nonalignment.

The neutrals affect the cold war in several ways. All of them attempt and many succeed in playing the two camps off against each other to their great profit in aid, flattery, and deference. They dominate the General Assembly of the United Nations; the questions discussed there today are a far cry from the power-political issues of the era of bipolarity. They show their distaste for great-power crisis and threats and offer support to any peaceful moves from either side. Both the Soviet and the United States have found it expedient to court their favor.

Americans have found it difficult, considering their view of the Soviet threat, to devise an effective approach to neutralism. The United States still seems to assume that the neutrals will eventually be won for the West. Neutralism is still considered by many as a transitory phenomenon that will disappear when full political maturity comes to the new states. In contrast to American reluctance to accept the reality of third-force elements in world politics, the Soviet acts as if it assumes neutralism to be permanent. It has actively sought to identify itself with many neutral causes, including disarmament, anticolonialism, and economic development. Only after Moscow began to score alarming successes did the United States attempt to recalculate its position.

THE SEARCH FOR NEW TECHNIQUES   After the stalemates in Korea and Indochina were made final after 1954 and the rise of neutralism certified the effective end of the pure bipolar era, America cast about for new ways of prosecuting the cold war. Containment had proved its virtues, but they were intrinsically limited ones. Some new rationale was needed if new types of struggle were to be undertaken.

This task has proved to be more difficult than expected. The United States has made an enormous investment in manpower, matériel, and prestige in the policy of bipolarity that foresees the eventual collapse of Soviet opposition and the complete vindication of the United States. Operationally, this view demands total hostility to the U.S.S.R. and a complete refusal to make any concessions to the Kremlin. The march of technology and the evolution of the world political system have effectively deprived the United States of the capacity to implement this approach. The nation has been committed to a version of victory that is simply unattainable under contemporary conditions.

Since 1954 the United States has had little success in finding new ways to fight the old cold war. Development assistance to new states and cultural exchanges with the U.S.S.R. are valuable enterprises, but they do not advance the nation any closer to a smashing victory over the Soviet. Probably the most significant new departure in American cold-war policy in recent years has been the prestige race with the Soviet, and the United States has presented to the world the unedifying spectacle of a great people obsessed with what others think of it and nervously comparing its image with that of its adversary.

Otherwise, the techniques of more recent American policy have been carryovers from the early bipolar era: security pacts, armaments, diplomatic warfare, and propaganda. The United States hopes to strengthen the free world in hopes of intimidating the Soviet; much recent thought has gone into planning for guerrilla ("counterinsurgency") assaults on Communist states. In the face of a drastically changed situation, America is attempting to meet the challenges of the present with the mental equipment and the techniques of the past.

THE ARMS RACE Adding a new dimension to the cold war after 1954 has been the arms race with the Soviet Union. As nuclear weapons and delivery systems in the form of missiles with ranges up to several thousand miles have been perfected, the two giants have competed in the development of massive armories of destructive capacity. Other states joined the contest, and by 1959 the nuclear club numbered four as Britain, followed by France, broke through. Others, including Communist China and several smaller nations, were on the very brink of doing so as the world moved into the 1960s.

The arms race had several implications. Each side rapidly developed what the Pentagon called "overkill" capability to destroy the other several times over. Paradoxically, the very destructiveness of the new weapons made their safe employment much less likely because of the great risk of retaliation. Weaponry thus became largely divorced from the implementation of national policy. The testing of nuclear devices polluted the atmosphere with radioactive fallout to some indefinite but measurable extent. The neutrals grew more and more perturbed about the possibility of a cataclysm that would engulf everyone.

In response to these considerations, after 1955 disarmament discussions—bogged down since 1949—were revived, although without success. In 1958 the U.S.S.R. unilaterally suspended further nuclear testing, the United States followed suit, and attention centered on attempts to formalize the moratorium into a permanent agreement to prohibit further testing. Negotiation went on for several years with no result, although the informal test ban remained in force. The Soviet feared espionage, the United States feared cheating; neither side would take the risk implicit in any agreement. In 1961 and 1962 the issue became sharp again as both major states resumed testing, this time of mammoth weapons of incalculable destructiveness.

In the meantime the arms race continued, driving up the risks of the cold war without increasing the chances of winning it. Neither side profited, but neither knew how to stop. The world watched, waited, and worried as the leaders maneuvered endlessly but without result.

THE NEGOTIATION OF THE COLD WAR   The evolution of the cold war during the latter fifties and early sixties pointed one clear moral for American policy. Barring some unforeseeable accident, the Soviet-American struggle was not destined to reach absolute resolution by any means short of holocaust; tension was to be America's lot for many years. In these terms a good argument could be made that the United States, instead of seeking always to increase the pressure on the U.S.S.R., would be better served to endeavor to reduce the intensity level of the cold war to a more bearable point.

Any such effort would require the elimination of at least some of the more nagging issues in East-West relations. Managing the cold war on a long-term basis is impossible without the diplomatic negotiation of differences in search of an acceptable compromise. This raises again the familiar dilemma of American policy. Serious negotiation with the Soviet demands a willingness to make some concessions to the Kremlin, and a corresponding agreeability on the part of the Soviet itself.

Both camps propagandize their willingness to negotiate issues, but except in a very few instances negotiation has not prospered in the cold war. The United States always discounts in advance any possibility of agreement by protesting Soviet bad faith and deceitfulness; it also takes the precaution of never including in its offers any of the points that the Soviet really wants. Moscow, of course, reciprocates, and has proved even more adept in confusing the diplomatic issues that lie between the two countries. The negotiation of the cold war seems like only a remote possibility when one looks at the world from an American point of view.

But both logic and history argue for the probability that at least some issues will soon be bargained over. Neither side can bear indefinitely to continue a struggle in which the disparity grows steadily greater between cost and effort on the one hand and positive results on the other. The spiral of frustration must be broken at some point; the cold war must eventually crest. One such catharsis would be nuclear war, but as long as leadership remains out of the hands of lunatics this is an outcome that will be avoided. No other way to step off the escalator can be found than all-out negotiation. Only if this fails should mankind reconcile itself to the worst.

The increasing reluctance of the neutrals passively to submit to manipulation in a pointless tug-of-war reinforces this trend. The non-Western world in particular may indeed hold the keys to the resolution of a stabilized cold war. They have already made clear their demand for a scaling back of the struggle; neutral pressure for real negotiation, already powerful, is destined to increase. The real test of the negotiability of cold-war issues, however, will come as each side begins the painful reassessment of its position that is a necessary preliminary to serious diplomacy.

THE FUTURE OF THE COLD WAR   After more than a decade and a half of struggle against the Soviet threat, Americans have been brought to an important turning point in their view of themselves and the world. The total victory that would release the tensions of twenty-odd years of crisis is now only a dream. The problem facing the nation today is that of developing a newly meaningful and more satisfying basis for conducting policy in an era of great and unpredictable change.

To the United States the cold war can in large measure be what Americans choose to make it. Up to the present the only justification needed for American action has been the inherent evil of the Soviet itself and the threat it has posed to the United States. Thus, American policy has too often been little more than a mirror image of Russian action: whatever Moscow has attempted Washington has sought to block. The psychological defensive on which the United States has placed itself was useful in inspiring reactions to Soviet pressure, but it has failed to generate a complementary set of positive purposes.

The future cold war will demand much more of the United States. America must stand for more than mere anti-Communism; the positive values in the American tradition must be rediscovered and made the basis for policy. Only in this way can the Soviet be brought to acceptable terms and the nature of American policy fully demonstrated to the world.

There has been little wrong with American cold-war techniques. American officials are by and large intelligent, dedicated, and energetic public servants. The frustration with which the nation has been gripped does not arise from any failure in will or execution. The problem lies in the blurring of the goals to which America is committed. No nation can know success unless it feels that the purpose it serves is real, immediate, and worthy. Awareness of this fact is the only real advantage the Soviet Union enjoys in the cold war.

The United States, therefore, must justify its future policy on the grounds of its own positive values and its own concrete purposes. Such a yardstick would not only revitalize the image of America about which so many are concerned today; it would also help develop the poise and self-confidence that has been lacking in recent American actions. These, coupled with the enormous human and material resources of the United States, provide ample reasons for Americans to face the future of the cold war with hope and confidence.

Review Questions

1. What is the American interpretation of the Soviet threat?

2. What are American cold-war goals?

3. What techniques does the United States use to build a strong free world bloc against the U.S.S.R.?

4. What are the direct anti-Soviet techniques used by the United States?

5. What is bipolarity? Why is it no longer relevant to the cold war?

6. Show how neutralism affects the cold war.

7. Why is the negotiation of cold-war issues becoming necessary?

MAJOR PROBLEMS OF FOREIGN POLICY TODAY

Chapter 6

The cold-war years have made abundantly clear one characteristic of international relations. For a great power, foreign-policy problems are never solved, but only lived with more or less comfortably. The United States, as it faces the latter decades of the twentieth century, can no longer afford to search for the "one right answer" to its problems. The world has grown too dangerous and too complex for any of the familiar formulas.

The international scene upon which the United States has been moving since the end of World War II has been marked by revolutionary change. From this unstable environment has flowed the Soviet challenge itself and also a family of other problems not inferior to the cold war in either importance or difficulty. A full perspective on the international role of the United States demands a serious evaluation of these as well.

FAMILIAR DILEMMAS

A first charge on continuing American effort consists of a group of very familiar dilemmas, spawned by the cold war and left hopelessly deadlocked during the years of Soviet-American struggle. So intertwined have they become with each other and with the overall positions of the two camps that there is a growing suspicion that only drastically changed approaches to them offer any promise of their eventual disposition.

EUROPEAN SECURITY   Probably the most deep-seated annoyance is that hardy perennial, the problem of a workable security system in Europe. Ever since the nineteenth-century concert of powers broke down on the eve of World War I, statesmen have wrestled fruitlessly with the complexities of European power relations. Europe in the cold-war era is no simpler to arrange than it was during the interwar years.

The Iron Curtain divides contemporary Europe, one part dominated by the Soviet and the other organized under American leadership. The two camps, each heavily armed, face each other across the grim barrier in almost total frustration. Neither side has been able to tilt the European balance in its favor; neither is satisfied with the situation, but neither dares release its grip to secure a better position. Each must content itself with moves to intensify the pressure on the other and to neutralize initiatives from the other side.

Obviously, in such a context "security" is an illusion. Since 1945, Europeans have known only an insecurity that has grown more acute as the consequences of breakdown have become more fearsome. It is no wonder that most of them watch great-power maneuvering with desperate fascination.

The United States identifies European security with a rollback of Soviet influence. Thus far, however, America has been unable to force Moscow either into a bargain or into a retreat. No security system for Europeans is possible unless Russians also feel secure, but American policy in Europe (NATO, German reunification, satellite liberation,

Western integration) is expressly designed to keep the Soviet off balance.

In recent years the Kremlin has undertaken several initiatives to re-open the entire European question, some coercive (the Berlin crises of 1959, 1961, and 1962), some negotiatory (disengagement and demilitarization in central Europe). In no case, however, has the United States shown any inclination to sacrifice any part of its position in return for a Soviet rollback; Washington professes to anticipate the day when Soviet collapse will win the entire American package at one blow. Meanwhile European security remains out of reach.

THE GERMAN PROBLEM The heart of the European dilemma is, of course, the status of Germany. The United States demands a Germany free, rearmed, reunited, and allied with the West, while the Soviet is determined to frustrate this aim and eventually to win all Germany for itself. In the meantime West Germany is a strong ally of the United States, while East Germany is a sullen and rebellious member of the Soviet bloc.

The German situation has changed little since the creation of the West German government in 1949. The West (backed by the Bonn government) calls for free elections for all Germany; Moscow demands negotiation between the two Germanies. Berlin—the weak spot in the Western position—is subject to Soviet blockade and pressure at any time.

The problem is complicated by Moscow's ability to grant reunification in return for a satisfactory arrangement with Bonn. The West must thus prevent any Soviet-German rapprochement. This in turn gives West Germany a powerful position in the Western camp and puts the United States often at Bonn's mercy. The fear of a new Soviet-German pact underlies a great deal of American policy.

The American policy toward Germany has been essentially short-range, concentrating on the integration of West Germany into the NATO bloc. In seeking to stabilize an admittedly insecure relationship, America has never squarely faced the issue of the ultimate destiny of Germany-in-Europe. As long as the cold war remains tense, the dangers of this approach will remain hidden; any sudden change in Soviet-American relations, however, will lay the United States open to a variety of risks. A position on Germany more inclusive than the current cold-war emphasis must be developed. The only question is whether it will be formulated in advance of a crisis or in the midst of rapidly moving events beyond American control.

THE SATELLITE NATIONS Also part of the baggage of the cold war is the matter of the Soviet satellites. Ever since 1945 the United States has "refused to accept" the enslavement of east Europe, and Americans all contemplate its eventual liberation. But ways to bring this about are difficult to find, and Soviet control in Eastern Europe has remained unshaken since the Hungarian rebellion in 1956.

The United States rejects military action as likely to precipitate total war. Merely to incite people to open rebellion against Soviet rule, however, invites ferocious reprisals. Subversion and guerrilla offensives are no more hopeful except to expatriate zealots. The U.S.S.R. obviously places a high priority on its grip in Eastern Europe, seeing in the satellites both a defensive buffer against Western aggression and an ideological vindication of its own position.

Thus Washington realizes that the liberation of the Soviet's European satellites can be accomplished only by negotiation. This requires not only Moscow's willingness to compromise its position, but also American offers of compensation attractive enough to tempt the Soviet. Here the German problem reasserts itself; only major modifications in the West's position on Germany could make the situation sufficiently fluid to open Eastern Europe to discussion. No such proposals have come from the United States, nor are any likely. The deadlock is complete.

In the meantime the United States contents itself with exploiting such minor freedom of action as the U.S.S.R. may grant any captive state. Some hopeful results have been obtained in the case of Poland; no success at all, however, has been enjoyed with the other satellites more under the Soviet's thumb. It seems clear that any change in Germany or Eastern Europe—short of a major war—will demand that they be attacked in some larger context than the cold war.

STALEMATE IN THE UNITED NATIONS The cold war has kept the Security Council of the United Nations completely helpless, but has left the General Assembly free to act. This body's instrument has been the Secretary-General. Recent trends within the United Nations threaten to extend the stalemate both to the General Assembly and to the Secretariat, a development that would not be an unmixed catastrophe to the United States but would undoubtedly pose serious problems.

The neutral bloc today can almost dominate the General Assembly.

The Soviet, seeking to capitalize on anti-Western biases, has sought a working alliance between its group and the neutrals. Its original project was the transformation of the Secretary-General's office into a troika of three, representing the Soviet bloc, the neutrals, and the West. Americans were dismayed over the prospect of a Soviet veto over all United Nations action, but usually overlooked the fact that the United States would receive the same veto power in return. Were the Soviet-neutral alignment to become a reality, Americans might well be grateful for such protection.

The United Nations has increasingly inhibited the freedom of action of both cold-war camps, and the real reason behind Moscow's moves may well be the hope of handcuffing the entire organization as effectively as is the Security Council. Since anticolonialist agitation frequently embarrasses the United States, an emasculated United Nations might free American hands for some forms of direct action presently thought inexpedient. Americans generally feel, however, that the United Nations has been a source of net advantage to the United States and condemn any diminution in its effectiveness.

The only way to ensure the frustration of Moscow's plan is for the United States to prevent the formation of the Soviet-neutral axis. This in turn demands enough American accommodation to the neutral bloc to keep them from the Soviet embrace. This has already proved a taxing and often annoying task, and it is bound to increase in complexity in the years ahead. Unless the United States is willing to forego the powerful force of the United Nations, however, no other course is possible.

THE NON-WESTERN REVOLUTION

The major change in the international system in the era since 1945 has been its conversion from a structure dominated by the states of Western culture into one in which the West finds itself in a distinct minority. The non-Western revolution has brought almost all peoples directly into international affairs. The new participants bring exotic cultures, different purposes, and new issues into the political arena. To the challenge of the new world the United States must bring as great a dedication as it has to the cold war.

THE REVOLT OF THE NON-WEST The non-Western revolution refers of course to much more than its most obvious manifestation, the liquidation of the great colonial empires of Britain, France, Belgium, the Netherlands, and Portugal. A complete overturn in world outlook and international behavior is sweeping the entire world outside Europe and Anglo-America. Africa, Asia, the Middle East, and Latin America are being shaken by a vast mass movement of multiple dimensions. Part of the revolution, it is true, is an urge for independence among all non-self-governing peoples; even among those states with a history of "independence," however, the trend of the times inspires them to seek larger international stature, fuller acceptance, and greater freedom of action and choice. The non-West now demands no less than complete political equality.

The revolt has its psychic overtones as well. Revenge for the indignities of colonialism and racism forms an important drive. The rising expectations that spark the movement obviously imply a mass demand for higher standards of living, featured by the creature comforts identified with Western life.

The non-Western revolt is a fruit of Western ideology. The doctrines of individual freedom and worth which in various forms (nationalism, capitalism, natural rights, etc.) have spurred the West for centuries have taken root throughout the world. In backward societies such ideas are explosive. The United States should take pride in knowing that the object lesson it affords to the world is the motivation for much of the shape and texture of the non-Western revolution. Communism, on the other hand, has very little to offer these revolutionaries except a dubious claim to greater speed.

NATIONALISM AND INDEPENDENCE The political manifestations of the non-Western revolution flow from the discovery of political identity and national self-consciousness among peoples everywhere. Western domination was feasible only as long as native populations remained passive and inert. World War II and modern technology, however, brought political sensitivity to the entire world. True political life was born.

Non-Western nationalism, new and unstable, takes many strange—often baffling—forms. It usually includes a fierce pride, a defiant insistence on independent action, and a delight in flaunting the symbols of national revival. In some cases it leads to attempts at dominance while in others to withdrawal. It tends to demand all the trappings of statehood, including especially armed forces, elaborate bureaucracies, and dazzling ceremonials. It is much more sensitive to slights and insults than are most of the older varieties.

Translated into policy, non-Western nationalism emphasizes freedom of choice and action. The states of the non-Western world, most of them small, weak, and at least potentially unstable, resent great-power domination and insist on making their own decisions. Most adopt neutrality in the cold war, not through ignorance of or suspended judgment on the issues, but because of their refusal to join any power blocs at all. They conduct their relations with the West as full status equals.

Although rent by bitter internal quarrels, the non-Western states recognize their common interest in resisting any new great-power control. In the United Nations, they are increasingly tending to coalesce to force the major states to scale back their own disagreements and to pay more attention to non-Western demands. Their success in this effort has been remarkable.

It is ironical that today those states most insistent on exercising nationalism and independent foreign policies are those with the least apparent capability to do so. World affairs, however, offers the non-West an unexpected opportunity that has been vigorously exploited. Non-Western nationalism pays off well.

RISING EXPECTATIONS The non-Western revolt is one of rising expectations. The peoples of the underdeveloped world have at last realized that poverty, disease, and misery are not inevitable. A large part of the dynamism of contemporary world politics stems from the demand of two-thirds of the world's population for material improvement in their conditions of life. This social urge immediately translates itself into concrete foreign policies by most of the governments concerned.

Non-Western states make the search for development assistance a major part of their approach. They are in a hurry, for rising expectations feed on themselves. The more popular demands are satisfied, the greater they become. Governments, themselves products of the very revolution they are leading, cannot delay providing the benefits their peoples demand without risking repudiation and replacement by other—possibly less responsible—political factions.

This has led many states to begin the dangerous but profitable game of playing one cold-war camp against the other. They seek assistance from both the Soviet bloc and the West, and count on mutual neutralization to leave them fully independent. This course has two dangers: that of miscalculation of the relative strength of the two sides and the loss of independence, and that of an unbalanced and ultimately self-destructive pattern of development that reaps a quick harvest of showy projects but fails to construct a sound basis for healthy economic life.

The promise of rapid results, however, continues to tempt leaders of many states to take the plunge.

So powerful has become the pressure for development and a higher standard of living that it must receive satisfaction of some sort. Its continued frustration in many parts of the world will ensure a variety of extremist adventures by reckless governments in search of quick solutions to long-standing dilemmas. The rise in expectations demands a comparable rise in fulfillment if stability is ever to come to the non-Western world. Societies of higher levels of development have in late years begun to explore seriously how this issue can be met squarely and rewardingly at a bearable cost and risk.

ANTICOLONIALISM   Anticolonialism is another familiar feature of the non-Western approach to the world. It has been most visible during the successful breakaways of one colony after another from European rule. Independence, however, does not extinguish anticolonialism in a non-Western society, but actually seems often to strengthen it. Non-Western states usually make a strong anticolonial position a fixed point in their foreign relations.

We must always remember that anticolonialism is indeed an "ism" with the hallmarks of any ideology. It not only attacks the illegality of alien rule over subject peoples, but its immorality as well. It makes a nation's stand on colonial questions the final test of its claim to respect, and argues that a past history of imperialism makes a country forever suspect unless it purge itself by becoming vehemently anticolonial itself in word and deed. Unfortunately but perhaps inevitably it has developed racist overtones that picture the white race as incessantly seeking to oppress all colored peoples.

All this is understandable enough. There is, however, another and equally important aspect to anticolonialism: It has proved to be very good politics. Much of the ex-imperial world has itself been disturbed about the moral implications of colonialism and is disposed to agree that both doctrine and practice should be completely discredited. This leads to a popular inclination to listen sympathetically to anticolonialist arguments, a situation very easy to turn to the direct advantage of the non-Western governments themselves.

Indeed, the United States has been handicapped by its intimate association with the leading colonial powers, while the U.S.S.R. has been vocal in its advocacy of the entire paraphernalia of anticolonialism. Paradoxically, non-Western states have usually received more real assistance—if less flamboyantly delivered—from the United States and its allies than from the Soviet bloc. But American uneasiness at the equivocal role the United States must play is obvious, and the nation finds itself frequently vulnerable to non-Western pressure applied in ways subtle or blunt but usually embarrassing.

THE NON-WEST AND THE COLD WAR   The non-Western revolution is a self-generating phenomenon, stemming from conditions and responses peculiar to the underdeveloped and anticolonialist world. It is not, in other words, a product of the cold war, is not controlled by either the Soviet or the Western bloc, and will not find its eventual resolution in cold-war terms. On the contrary, it has already exerted great influence on the context of the Soviet-American struggle, and will probably have a marked effect on its long-term future.

Generally speaking, the emerging nations do not accept an ideological formulation of the cold war, but see it as another in the long series of great-power disputes inherent in international politics. This is not to suggest that they see no difference between the antagonists or that they are indifferent to the possible consequences of a Soviet victory. They do not, however, believe that the struggle is one between absolute good and absolute evil, nor do they feel compelled to subordinate their own immediate interests to the overriding task of bringing victory to one side or the other. They see no attraction or utility in a bipolar view of the world.

Instead they accept the cold war as an important and relatively fixed condition of international existence, to be coped with and taken advantage of when possible. Neutralism—nonalignment—has proved feasible for many as a basic posture, at least in Asia, the Middle East, and Africa; Latin America has been neither so eager nor as able to break with its cold-war orientation. But mere abstention from great-power maneuvering is not enough. Most non-Western states seek a working policy to capitalize on their lack of commitments. This is the province of what is often called "positive" neutralism.

A state playing the game of positive neutralism carries on an active policy of negotiation with both cold-war camps. By playing them against each other, it gains far more in material aid and augmented power and status than it could ever hope for by open adherence to either. Although both major blocs resent treating young, small, and often irresponsible states with exaggerated deference and solicitude, they find themselves open to neutralist pressures. Neither dares allow the other a clear field in any region, while both hope finally to win these states for their cause. Shrewd neutrals have developed great skill in leading on both Moscow and Washington in this latter ambition.

In spite of their dexterity in walking the dangerous and narrow path between the giants, however, most non-Western states genuinely fear any escalation of the cold war. They have no wish to lose their bargaining position through any sudden relaxation in Soviet-American tensions, but they would much prefer that the struggle be carried on in a less perilous atmosphere. The general non-Western approach, therefore, favors disarmament and greater use of United Nations procedures to minimize tensions, but is seldom explicit about methods of removing the grounds of dispute between the Soviet Union and the West.

THE UNITED STATES AND THE NON-WESTERN REVOLUTION   Equipped neither by temperament nor by historical experience to cope quickly with the non-Western world, the United States has experienced serious difficulty in developing an effective approach. The steady increase in the global role of the underdeveloped states has alerted Americans to the necessity of coming meaningfully to grips with the problem they present. Before a workable policy atmosphere can be developed, however, certain persistent American misjudgments must be corrected.

The first and most pervasive American misapprehension has been the interpretation of the non-Western revolution in cold-war terms. This creates the assumption that any revolution is at least potentially Communist and has focused American attention on only a few countries in which "crisis" has been well publicized (outstanding examples, of course, include Cuba, Laos, and the Congo). On the other hand, equally significant revolutionary forces have been overlooked in areas where the "Communist menace" is less obvious. The American search for pro-Western and pro-Communist elements in each revolution has led to one error and embarrassment after another.

Part of this same pattern, but distinct in its application, is the false assumption that the neutralism of the non-Western world is a transitory phase in its evolution toward final adherence to the Western bloc. The United States still hopes to harvest a crop of cold-war allies among the emerging nations once they appreciate the iniquity of Soviet behavior and the disinterested quality of American motives. Thus, the United States still attaches political strings to aid programs and to obstruct Soviet-neutral relations. Few American programs have been less successful, and few have earned more enmity.

A third failure in American understanding has been an overemphasis on the economic and social aspects of the revolution and a corresponding underestimate of its political and psychic dimensions. The United States seems to feel that the achievement of a higher standard of living by an underdeveloped people will quiet them down and liquidate their dynamism. History and logic both testify to the fallacy of this easy formula. The revolution itself has its roots in a mass emotional awakening, and can never run its course until these original emotions are satisfied. The behavior of the new states has proved beyond doubt that their real goal is not simply greater material comfort for their peoples, but rather the attainment of status, deference values, and dignity equal with the West. Economic aid without this psychic component, far from eliminating the problem, often only intensifies it.

Americans, whose contact with the exotic cultures of the non-Western world has usually been via missionaries or salesmen, tend overwhelmingly to adopt an attitude of well-meaning patronage in dealing with the new states. With the best will imaginable, Americans consider non-Western societies to be not only technically backward—which they usually are—but also politically unsophisticated, culturally barren, emotionally immature, and vulnerable to Communist wiles. Such people, America argues, must be dealt with as adolescents, to be humored, led firmly, occasionally chastised, but never taken seriously. Almost as unfortunate is the opposite tendency among other equally sincere citizens who virtually "go native" in their enthusiasm for non-Western virtues and who earn only contempt instead of the resentment inevitable in the wake of the first judgment.

One remaining error should be mentioned: the assumption among militant cold warriors that the non-Western world is of little importance to the United States because of its almost total lack of military power. The revolt of the non-West is dismissed as no more than an irrelevant digression from the main business of the nation. The United States, if only it would muster the "will" to do so, could reverse the tide of anticolonialism and restore Asia, Africa, the Middle East, and Latin America to the wise and just control of the West. This dangerous illusion, popular with political and military leaders of a generally conservative orientation, is usually linked to a fixation on NATO as the core of American policy. It seems hardly necessary to point out that any attempt to follow this policy would produce only disaster. In point of fact, the importance of the non-Western world grows largely from its very lack of armed force. Open coercion of any non-Western state would bring down the organized wrath of the remainder of the world on the United States and go far toward giving cold-war victory finally to the Soviet Union.

It would be futile to suggest any overall American approach to the non-Western revolution. In spite of its essential unity, it presents too many different problems to be amenable to any single technique. If the United States, however, were to correct the errors and misjudgments it has been making and accept the necessity of dealing with this enormous movement in its own terms, the outlines of a workable policy would not be difficult to discover. The revolt of two-thirds of the world is so awe-inspiring and portentous a phenomenon that living with it with any satisfaction demands generous amounts of clarity, vision, and intelligence.

ARMS CONTROL AND DISARMAMENT

The continued evolution of military technology toward the point of absolute destructiveness has kept alive the problem of controlling and if possible reducing armaments through the darkest days of the cold war. The urgency of the question is underscored by the baleful prospect of a nuclear war and its horrifying aftermath. The United States, unable up to this point to develop a clear position or an effective policy on arms control, has not by its hesitation in any way escaped the necessity of making the hard choices called for. If not in the past, then in the future Americans must face the implications of where the arms race is taking the world.

THE PROBLEMS   The central problem is an old one: armaments are tools of state action, and no state will voluntarily strip itself of any instrument it feels it might require. Thus, arms limitation can take place only in an atmosphere of relative security as states divest themselves of weapons they deem surplus. Since 1945 no such climate of decision has existed in world politics.

There has remained only the prospect of conflict. Each side discusses arms control only to load upon the other the blame for failure or, as an outside possibility, to attempt to trap the other into an agreement that will confer a political-military advantage. Considering the skill both sides have developed in this pointless exercise, it is no wonder that the record of disarmament discussions is one of unbroken futility.

Complicating the situation is the continuing arms race. Arms competition in the nuclear age is more qualitative than quantitative, more a matter of developing new kinds of weapons than of increasing the numbers of old ones. One of the most telling arguments against a ban on nuclear testing, and the fact that led both sides to resume testing after 1961, was the danger that military technology would freeze unless new developments were tested. The possibility of a technological breakthrough into absolute military dominance is the will-o'-the-wisp that energizes the arms race.

One final aspect of the arms control problem adds its quota of perplexity: the so-called "nth power" issue. Nuclear weapons are great equalizers. Once a state gains nuclear capability it is substantially equal with all great states. When nuclear weapons are developed by small and irresponsible states, the dangers of catastrophe are multiplied many times. The great powers are anxious to develop a control system before they lose all their ability to dominate events.

THE ISSUES   There are dozens of issues implicit in arms negotiations, but a few can be distinguished as basic. Perhaps most important is the goal: Is it *control*, in which the use of arms is inhibited but their amounts left unlimited, or a real *reduction* of armaments (no one in the West takes really seriously any proposal for total *disarmament*)? American policy has swung slowly from an advocacy of reduction to one of control, exactly as the Soviet has done the opposite. These swings coincide roughly with the rise in Soviet military technology.

A second issue concerns the relative risks involved either in a workable control system or an uncontrolled and intensified arms race. The United States, partly through distrust of Soviet intentions and partly to preserve its own freedom of action, has consistently felt the risk of arms competition to be more bearable than that of control. It has therefore been unwilling to give up very much to gain Soviet agreement to a system the nation itself feels is of dubious value.

Inherent in this crisis of decision is a judgment of the real utility of military power under contemporary technological conditions. The strategic stalemate—the balance of terror—grips both sides today; from one point of view most weapons might be classified as politically surplus. But both tradition and the hope of decisive military advantage inhibit attempts at action. Military establishments grow more and more elaborate as opportunities for their safe use become more rare.

A final issue is the question of the role in arms control to be played by the world at large. There is no such thing as a private war with nuclear weapons. Much of mankind, speaking through the United Nations, insists both on an end to the spiraling arms race and on its right to participate in the act of control. The major camps are not receptive, preferring to keep their military relationships a matter between themselves. The U.S.S.R. has gone somewhat further than the United States in adapting itself, at least for propaganda purposes, to neutral demands.

THE PROSPECTS   No one can be certain about the prospects for arms control, although everyone agrees that some real relief from the pressures of the arms race would be a blessing. All the world really knows about arms reduction, however, are certain of its essential prerequisites.

In the first place, real and effective arms control cannot take place except within a political context. It is useless to seek any agreement in a vacuum. No state will accept limits on its ability to defend itself or make war except as part of a larger resolution of conflicts. This does not imply that arms control is impossible unless preceded by or coupled with political settlements, since a disarmament agreement might well be the first step in a major *détente*. But it is vital to view the entire subject of arms control in a political rather than a narrow military or technological light. The basic risks to be assumed are themselves political, and only political calculations can determine if the gains to be won are worth the costs.

A second prerequisite for arms control is a realization that no acceptable foolproof (or "cheatproof") system can be devised. Any agreement must be founded on the assumption of good faith by all parties, however difficult it might be to justify. Arms limitation is a voluntary act, and no government will risk such self-denial unless it feels others will do the same. Control systems, inspections, reports, and publicity may be useful, but in the last analysis there is only one technique of "enforcement" of predictable value: national interest. The search for ways to coerce adherence to an arms control agreement—at least within the nation-state system—is foredoomed to failure. All it can do is to turn up countless arguments against making any agreement at all, a purpose not without merit but unfortunately not one that provides any escape from arms competition and the upward spiral of disaster.

Finally, an arms control system must provide acceptable alternative techniques of state action. No state will forego useful capability unless it is confident that it can achieve enough of its objectives by other means. The absolute victory of war must be replaced by the relative victories of peaceful change. Participants in an arms control agreement do not abandon their disputes, but only place limits on the methods they will use in prosecuting them. One important test of the workability of any such arrangement will be whether the states involved feel it allows them enough room to act usefully. Arms control cannot be used to freeze international relations.

WILL AMERICA MEET THE TEST?

Implicit in all discussion of foreign policy in the United States today is the most fundamental issue of all: Will America (and Americans) meet and successfully surmount the tests the world is imposing? For a nation whose sense of mission and self-confidence were known world-wide for decades, it might seem odd to raise such a question, evoking doubt as it does about the very survival of the United States. Yet the Communists are not alone in predicting the decline and ultimate fall of American civilization; friendly critics and many Americans as well are concerned about the possibility of defeat. There has been abroad in the United States a deep if only half-articulated distrust of the nation's ability to cope with its problems.

Because the vigor of American action depends to a major extent upon America's own estimate of its capability to act effectively, it is critical that the United States deliberately and finally persuade itself that the challenges it will face are within its ability to turn back. Americans must believe that the problems are indeed soluble in some satisfactory way, or else there is little point in making any effort at all. This con- clusion is neither sentimental nor unscientific, but merely self-evident. No nation can survive without a sustained faith in itself to provide the necessary fulcrum for action.

FOREIGN POLICY AND DEMOCRACY   Probably the central problem that must be resolved before Americans can fully rationalize their position in the world is a satisfactory reconciliation of the requirements of foreign policy with the code and the practice of democracy. There is a good deal of evidence supported by cogent arguments that contends that by its very nature foreign affairs is an undemocratic enterprise and that it is literally impossible to blend the demands for expertise, secrecy, com- promise, and amoral and realistic analysis with the democratic traits of publicity, controversy, proliferation of special interests, and pandering to the least common denominator of mass prejudices, fears, and appe- tites. No issue could more clearly put democratic processes to the test;

if a democratic foreign policy is impossible, then national survival may well demand the abandonment of the most fundamental principles on which the nation was founded.

Without attempting to exhaust an obviously large subject, we may suggest several points that bear on this issue and that may provide some escape from the dilemma. In the first place, many of the strictures against foreign policy in a democracy misplace the role of popular government on basic issues. It would be idiotic to suggest that mass referenda could replace the expert judgments of professional foreign-policy personnel, and no such intimate mass role is indeed necessary. If the public plays its appropriate role—if, in other words, it focuses on the value choices that we noted in Chapter 1 as lying at the bottom of all foreign-policy decisions—and if these underlying goals and objectives are communicated to the leadership, then the crucial elements of democracy are retained.

Even in these limited terms, however, the American public has not been playing its part adequately. Either through apathy, complacency, or anxiety (all three have been suggested), the quality of mass discussion and response has been disappointing throughout the entire postwar era. Unable or unwilling to agree on goals, to make the necessary basic choices, or to learn enough facts, *"homo Americanus"* has preferred generally to indulge his hates and fears, to prefer a negative reaction to a positive one, and to substitute the manipulation of stale formulas for serious discussion. It has been this failure of the ultimate trustees of democracy to come up to the mark that has touched off so much doubt among serious analysts about the survival value of democracy in a world of crisis.

THE ROLE OF LEADERSHIP   It is by now a cliché that modern democracy is a function of leadership, and that this is especially true in matters of foreign policy. Only expert and politically responsible leaders can make and execute foreign affairs with the requisite efficiency. It is the group of leaders, furthermore, who shape and direct mass responses to events and who control the consensus that supports government action.

If this formulation be accurate (and most scholars agree that it is), then the somewhat surprising conclusion suggests itself that to a great extent the low state of popular morale and insight on international questions in the United States is the fault of the leadership itself. At various points in the preceding pages we have had occasion to note certain characteristics of contemporary American policy: its rigidity, its simplistic formulations, its negativism. Official leadership must share responsibility for this state of affairs with an unsophisticated and emotion-filled public.

Admittedly, the years since 1945 have been filled with crises to which several generations of leaders have felt called on to respond. Pressed for time and without the opportunity for leisurely analysis, these policy makers have repeatedly taken the easy way out by pressing the "panic button" of mass concern. Rather than risk a full-dress debate, official-dom has normally wrapped issue after issue in the cloak of crisis and won support from the mass. But they have paid a price; as problems grow increasingly subtle and complex, their past record of whetting popular appetite for bold action in the face of danger inhibits their freedom to act otherwise.

Before the full strength of an appropriately concerned and ade-quately educated mass public can be thrown behind a foreign policy appropriate to America's real world role, national leadership circles and their affiliated elites must face the necessity of undertaking long-range programs of public education about the real nature of foreign policy. The world of the future will be less and less responsive to the extemporized but stubbornly defended policies upon which the United States has relied so often in the past.

By "public education" is meant little more than a simple but far-reaching change in the way in which leadership sets the tone of public discussion. When Washington ceases to formulate problems in dichoto-mous (and usually misleading or irrelevant) terms, but instead lets the public discuss problems in terms of the same range of alternatives the decision makers themselves perceive, the quality—as well as the quantity—of public response will increase. When (to put it bluntly) the body of officials allow the mass of the people, operating at a lower level of technical competence but secure in their grasp of the value issues involved, to participate meaningfully in shaping at least the outlines of policy, both the effectiveness of American action and the vitality of American democracy will be reinforced.

A crucial role in this process can be played by the so-called "elite public": that relatively small percentage of the population that has ac-quired enough skill in analysis and communication to converse intelli-gently with the decision makers on the one hand and with the mass on the other. If brought into the communication pattern early and extensively, these comparatively competent laymen of various sorts can be of central importance in transmitting official formulations to cen-

ters of discussion and in helping to shape and direct the ensuing consensus. Also critical are the undifferentiated "opinion leaders," difficult
to identify but vital in the multistage flow of messages from the leadership to the mass.

THE CRISIS OF VALUES   We close by restating a point with which we
began this book. It is a truism of politics that a people receives the
quality of government they expect and demand. In the last analysis,
American foreign policy and the men who make and execute it are
the servants of a set of mass expectations and demands. No leadership
can be any better than the task to which it is set by its people.

So, even after granting the existence and the inescapability of the
limits on American action set by the world system itself and by the
shortcomings in the government and political structure in the United
States, it remains true that a marked improvement is possible in American foreign policy. Whether or not this happy development occurs, however, is in the hands of the American people at large. Before their
leaders can move the country, the country must be willing to move.

This is not to suggest that America must become a nation of foreign-
policy experts. It will be ample ground for substantial new departures
in policy if only the public meets the principal responsibility it has been
neglecting: the recreation of a workable value consensus. If, in other
words, American life again comes to demonstrate agreement upon the
key notions of public and private good and the (perhaps utopian)
mission Americans see themselves performing in the world, the cur-
rently frustrating task of policy making will be drastically simplified.
Such a rediscovery of a value system and such an implicit rededication
of the nation to a positive purpose can only come through the mechanisms of mass consensus. No elite or no leader can create them.

The free society and political system Americans enjoy are the fruits
of a deliberate gamble that individuals, given a relatively broad range
of free choice, will choose correctly enough of the time to enable the
system to survive. The world challenge today is the most serious one
Americans have ever faced. It demands more knowledge, courage, confidence, efficiency, and persistence than the nation has ever before been
called on to produce. The real challenge the United States faces is
whether the vision of the free man in the open society can be made
to stand up in a world grown complex and menacing. With the price
of failure so great, Americans must now demonstrate that they have the
wisdom to determine the right course and the courage to follow it.

Review Questions

1. What are the major elements in current American policy in Europe?

2. How has the United States reacted to the stalemate in the United Nations?

3. What are the major elements in the non-Western revolution? How has the United States coped with this revolution?

4. What has been United States policy relative to neutralism among the non-Western states? To anti-colonialism?

5. What are the leading issues in the question of arms control? What are the prerequisites for an agreement?

For Further Reading

ALMOND, GABRIEL A.: *The American People and Foreign Policy*, Harcourt, Brace & World, Inc., New York, 1950.

BAILEY, THOMAS A.: *A Diplomatic History of the American People*, 6th ed., Appleton-Century-Crofts, Inc., New York, 1958.

BEMIS, SAMUEL F.: *A Diplomatic History of the United States*, 4th ed., Holt, Rinehart and Winston, Inc., New York, 1955.

BLOOMFIELD, LINCOLN W.: *The United Nations and U.S. Foreign Policy*, Little, Brown and Company, Boston, 1960.

CERF, JAY H., and WALTER POZEN (eds.): *Strategy for the 60s*, Frederick A. Praeger, Inc., New York, 1961.

CLAUDE, INIS L.: *Swords Into Plowshares*, 2d ed., Random House, Inc., New York, 1959.

COHEN, BERNARD C.: *The Political Process and Foreign Policy*, Princeton University Press, Princeton, N.J., 1957.

COMMISSION ON NATIONAL GOALS: *Goals for Americans*, Prentice-Hall, Inc., Englewood Cliffs, N.J., 1960.

DE CONDE, ALEXANDER: *The Secretary of State*, Frederick A. Praeger, Inc., New York, 1962.

ELDER, ROBERT: *The Policy Machine*, Syracuse University Press, Syracuse, N.Y., 1961.

ETZIONI, MARIO: *The Hard Way to Peace*, Collier Books, a division of Crowell-Collier Publishing Co., New York, 1962.

FINLETTER, THOMAS K.: *Foreign Policy: the Next Phase, the 1960's*, Frederick A. Praeger, Inc., New York, 1960.

FROMM, ERICH: *May Man Prevail?* Doubleday & Company, Inc., Garden City, N.Y., 1961.

GOLDMAN, ERIC F.: *The Crucial Decade and After: America 1945–1960*, Alfred A. Knopf, Inc., New York, 1960.

HAVILAND, H. FIELD: *The Formulation and Administration of United States Foreign Policy*, The Brookings Institution, Washington, 1960.

HERO, ALFRED O.: *Americans in World Affairs*, World Peace Foundation, Boston, 1959.

KAHN, HERMAN: *On Thermonuclear War*, Princeton University Press, Princeton, N.J., 1960.

KENNAN, GEORGE F.: *American Diplomacy, 1900–1950*, The University of Chicago Press, Chicago, 1951.

KISSINGER, HENRY A.: *The Necessity for Choice*, Harper & Row, Publishers, Incorporated, New York, 1960.

———: *Nuclear Weapons and Foreign Policy*, Harper & Row, Publishers, Incorporated, New York, 1957.

KNORR, KLAUS (ed.): *NATO and American Security*, Princeton University Press, Princeton, N.J., 1959.

LEFEVER, ERNEST W. (ed.): *Arms and Arms Control*, Frederick A. Praeger, Inc., New York, 1962.

LERCHE, CHARLES O., JR.: *Foreign Policy of the American People*, 2d ed., Prentice-Hall, Inc., Englewood Cliffs, N.J., 1961.

LIPPMANN, WALTER: *The Public Philosophy*, Little, Brown and Company, Boston, 1955.

MACMAHON, ARTHUR W.: *Administration in Foreign Affairs*, University of Alabama Press, University, Ala., 1953.

MILLIKAN, MAX F. (ed.): *The Emerging Nations*, Little, Brown and Company, Boston, 1961.

MILLIS, WALTER, et al.: *A World Without War*, Washington Square Press, Pocket Books, Inc., New York, 1962.

MORGENTHAU, HANS J.: *Politics Among Nations*, 3d ed., Alfred A. Knopf, Inc., New York, 1960.

———: *The Purpose of American Politics*, Alfred A. Knopf, Inc., New York, 1960.

PRATT, JULIUS W.: *A History of United States Foreign Policy*, Prentice-Hall, Inc., Englewood Cliffs, N.J., 1955.

PRICE, DON K. (ed.): *The Secretary of State*, Prentice-Hall, Inc., Englewood Cliffs, N.J., 1960.

ROBINSON, JAMES: *Congress and Foreign Policy*, The Dorsey Press, Homewood, Ill., 1962.

ROSTOW, WALT W.: *The United States in the World Arena*, Harper & Row, Publishers, Incorporated, New York, 1960.

SCHUMAN, FREDERICK L.: *International Politics*, 6th ed., McGraw-Hill Book Company, Inc., New York, 1960.

SPANIER, JOHN W.: *American Foreign Policy Since World War II*, rev. ed., Frederick A. Praeger, Inc., New York, 1962.

STRAUSZ-HUPÉ, ROBERT, et al.: *A Forward Strategy for America*, Harper & Row, Publishers, Incorporated, New York, 1961.

TANNENBAUM, FRANK: *The American Tradition in Foreign Policy*, University of Oklahoma Press, Norman, Okla., 1955.

WESTERFIELD, BRADFORD W.: *Foreign Policy and Party Politics*, Yale University Press, New Haven, Conn., 1955.

Index